The Doll Book

The
Doll Book

SOFT DOLLS AND CREATIVE FREE PLAY

KARIN NEUSCHÜTZ

Translated from the Swedish
Lek Med Mjuka Dockor
by Ingun Schneider

Larson

Illustrations: Karin Neuschütz
Cover photos: Lars Larsson

Manufactured in the U.S.A.

Library of Congress
Catalogue Card Number: 82-17094

First published 1979 in Sweden as
Lek med mjuka dockor. Translated
into English by Ingun Schneider.

Published by
LARSON PUBLICATIONS, INC.
4936 Route 414, Box 79A
Burdett, New York 14818

10 9 8 7 6 5 4 3 2

Contents

1

Introduction

Everything went wrong on this beautiful summer day. The children couldn't play; they just fought over their things. So we went on an excursion to find raspberries instead. We left all our belongings, just took a pail and went off.

When we reached the raspberry patch the children were happy again. Once they had stuffed themselves full of berries, the playing could begin.

My older child found a dry old tree branch in the ditch: "Oh, look, here's a factory! Come here and see all the long pipes. What's floating in the pipes?"

"Raspberry juice, of course!" my younger child said.

Then they got stones to use as trucks and transported some raspberries which they crushed and pretended to pour into the twigs on the branch. Little sticks became workers who were rushing here and there.

The children laughed and showed me the remarkable factory; they were as proud as if they had made a revolutionary invention.

Well, hadn't they?

They had actually created a whole raspberry-factory out of almost nothing. They had made themselves very simple little models of people—as children have done throughout history. A little piece of wood or a stone becomes alive and walks around—the very simplest of dolls.

Children often have such strong imagination and ability to play that they prefer simple and natural things instead of their fancy toys. They pretend to be the mother of a pillow wrapped in a scarf; they tie a string around a crinkled-up newspaper and drag it around like a dog.

The ambitious parent who invested so much to give his child fancy toys stands back and feels disillusioned!

Once my children adopted a piece of wood, named it Harvey, and lovingly tucked it into the doll carriage. The cloth doll I had sewn for them was mercilessly dumped out of the carriage and remained on the floor! Now it was Harvey that needed their loving attention.

The children aren't playing to make me happy. They don't play with things I've given them or made for them just because it would be impolite to let them lie there unused. No, they play because they have to play.

Playing is one way children can grow and develop. Through play, children prepare for their lives as adults. To see what something feels like and to get a taste of it for themselves, they pretend to be mother or father, traveling, shopping.

Therefore I mustn't be hurt when my doll lies forgotten on the floor while Harvey, the piece of wood, is dressed in the doll's sweater. Instead, I'm happy that their imagination is so powerful as to even resist my influence!

After a period of time, Harvey was suddenly tossed into the fireplace and burned up! At that moment he became a regular piece of wood. When my child saw me put other pieces of wood into the fire, she tossed Harvey in also.

"Oh, Harvey got burned up!" she noted calmly.

"But, he'll come back soon," she comforted herself.

"I'm sure he will," I said, figuring that there are many pieces of wood or pillows that can become new dolls. But my daughter looked for her soft cloth doll; now she apparently needed it again.

Why do children so often choose such strange objects to use in their play? Why don't they just take the beautiful, ready-made things that we give them? Perhaps the reason is that children want to use their own lively imagination. They want to create by themselves; they don't want to just "consume." If they have all kinds of material available—paper, crayons, empty boxes, fabric, blankets, pieces of wood and leather, pillows—and if they can use some pieces of furniture as building material, they can find places to build raspberry-juice factories anywhere.

If they receive toys in which characteristic gestures and features are only suggested, there is room for their own imagination to add what is missing.

Nourishing their imagination during childhood can have an influence on how they perform their tasks as adults and on their attitude toward and involvement with their fellow men.

Through play the child enters life

As soon as the healthy child has learned something new, it starts to play with the new ability—practicing and testing. As the child develops, it tackles more and more difficult tasks. The child who has just learned to walk takes little dance-steps; the child who can talk sings and rattles nonsense words. If she can dress herself, she starts to dress up or to put the clothes on wrong just for fun.

The three-year-old who has recently understood that he is "I" pretends that he is someone else—a little mouse that squeaks, or a baby. He is testing the limits of his own "I" by changing roles.

As soon as the child has learned a few activities of the home and knows what rugs and furniture are used for, it recreates and transforms the everyday into an adventure: the rug is an island, the floor an ocean, the easy chair a rowboat. The shades are drawn and day becomes night.

The shades go up and it's morning already.

The child practices all skills through rhythmic repetition. The child enters life through play. And all the time its eyes follow the grown-ups in their activities—for one day he or she will also get big.

The five-to-six-year-old child's consciousness has expanded to the extent that it can get an overview of larger contexts. It is interested in the reason why we do the things we do, and it becomes more purposeful in its own activities. Everything the child meets is worked through during play. Whole worlds appear. The child plays school, hospital, family, theater. The child imagines what the adults do, what life "is all about."

At about the age of seven comes a release of much energy that the child previously needed to control and to come to terms with its body. This creative energy now benefits the imagination. Memory gets developed; the child can see "inside the head" and also thinks into the future. The consciousness of time also becomes more developed.

During school-age games that follow, rules begin and the children practice coordinating themselves with others.

The nine-to-ten-year-olds are collectors; wanting to figure out how it is organized, they look out into our big world. Remarkable machines are constructed, houses are drawn in cross section, factories and communications systems are developed. The child develops its own interests, becomes a specialist, collects facts. Now the child feels "big," starts to criticize the adults, makes caricatures of them, and gets into mischief. Now the child "officially" stops playing.

The young child's imagination is busy developing the physical body. Its imagination is actually needed for the growing and shaping of the organism.

These imagination-forces are then released as the child turns six or seven and is more comfortable with the body. As these forces are no longer needed for growing and forming, they can be transformed into soul-activities, into creativity and sensitivity.

Out of this living imagination come the mental abilities, the clarity of thought, and the power of ideas in the teenager.

So much for an abbreviated description of how the child plays through the ages.

But there are children who can't play, who don't want to or don't have the energy to play, or who just rush and run around without being happy with what they are doing. How can we help them?

I think that we always have to start with ourselves when we are trying to discover the reasons for a child's disharmony. Our own state of being is the well from which the children draw inspiration and joy of living. They hover near us in all that they do; they want to be like us in every way. To guide our children we must therefore start by attending to ourselves. If the people around the child are happy and active, the child will be also.

Taking the time to slowly and peacefully make a doll for the child can be a nice way to get close to him or her. As I sit and sew, I think about the child who will have this doll. The child certainly senses the love and care that I "sew into" the doll.

In this book I describe my own experiences of how children play at different ages, of how they are affected by their surroundings and by the people around them. My views have slowly arisen through work with my own and others' children. I have learned a lot from my own childhood memories and through studies of child psychology and pedagogy—mainly works by Rudolf Steiner and many of his followers. I have picked up many things from today's Waldorf (Rudolf Steiner) schools and have tried to synthesize all this into a uniform whole.

I want to direct many warm thanks to Gisela Richert, who initiated me into the art of making soft dolls.

Finally, I want to emphasize that the dolls described in the book's second half are regular yarn or cloth dolls that have been made by hand in many parts of the world. The Waldorf pedagogy cannot claim the sole honor of these dolls, for they have existed in many other circumstances. They are, however, gladly used in the Waldorf kindergartens, and my hope is that they will exist in most homes of the future!

Eric is 45 cm. (17¾ in.) tall, and his hair is naturally dyed with tansy. His mother said one day, "You know that dolls are such mini-babies because their mommies are mini-mommies!"

She was obviously pleased with the size comparison.

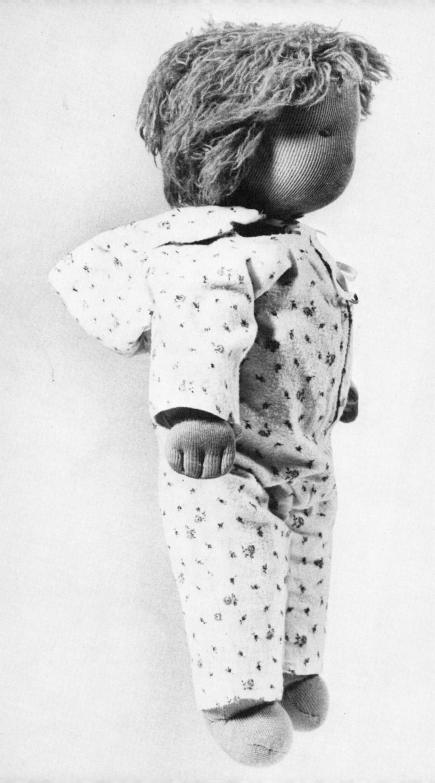

Soft dolls

The picture shows a knot-doll. The knot-doll is versatile, for it is so simple that you can vary it endlessly.

It can be made of paper, fabric, leather, or straw. It can be made small or large. It can have arms and legs, hair and clothes according to the child's desire.

Using simply a square piece of material and a little wool or fleece for the head, you can tie a first doll for the infant. You can entertain the child on a car ride, in a waiting room, etc., by improvising different knot-dolls with a handkerchief.

It's almost impossible to map the history of the rag doll.
At archaeological diggings all kinds of finds are made—but
how is one to judge whether the little piece of cloth and the
piece of wood was a beloved doll or just a rag and some wood?

Dolls have been made throughout history. Before man had
any tools to work with, he probably just took a stone or a
piece of wood that had the shape of a human being. The simple, improvised dolls were the favorites. They were played
with until they went to pieces, and few of them were left for
posterity. Therefore, the history of dolls is mostly a chron-
icle of beautiful and fancy dolls which date from but a few
centuries back.

During the sixteenth, seventeenth, and eighteenth centuries,
dolls were often made of wood, wax, or papier-maché. They
often had a layer of wax over the face to give a melancholic
expression and a shiny skin. (The poor child who got too close
to the hot stove with the doll!)

These fancy dolls had a real heyday during the 1800s—especially in France, where the large clothiers used dolls with
elegant wardrobes as models.

Nineteenth-century dolls were made of porcelain (unglazed
porcelain was called bisque) or of a mass consisting of plaster, bran, and leather. They often had thin, gracious, adult
shapes.

By 1827 there were already dolls that could say "mama."
There were even dolls that could "breathe."

Eventually the "uncrushable" celluloid and the first plastic
appeared and radically changed the conditions for doll-mak-
ing. When dolls could be mass-produced, they became so
inexpensive that every home could have one. Previously,
poor families had perhaps been able to afford one porcelain
doll head—to which they sewed a body.

In most homes that had a fancy store-bought doll, the children played with homemade dolls. The fancy doll sat high up
on a shelf in the parlor—majestic and untouchable. It was admired by visitors and was only taken down at special occasions.
The children did not get to play with that doll unless the family
was unusually well off. Instead, they would stand and dream
and fantasize about the remarkable beauty on the shelf.

I wonder if many of these fancy dolls weren't secretly taken down by the children when the parents weren't nearby? Children in all cultures have probably secretly played with the little house-god, the fetish, the saint-figure, the sculpture. They were all important adult "dolls" and were therefore numinous in the children's eyes.

Then came the plastic dolls. Suddenly there was an excess of them. The adults didn't value them particularly much, and they became typical babies of the nursery. If the doll broke you bought a new one.

The inexpensive plastic and rubber dolls replaced both the fancy dolls on the shelf and the homemade rag dolls. Then the adults didn't have to make any more dolls for the children—just like they soon won't have to sing songs for them (since there are records!) or tell stories (since radio and TV have story hours!).

20

But maybe the tradition of making dolls in the home has only temporarily ceased. Perhaps it will reawaken through the need felt by so many adults to be creative and to enter into hobby activities.

Dress-up dolls similar to the one described on page 130 were made at the turn of this century in the countryside homes of Switzerland, Germany, and other countries. As these dolls matched their own ideas of how suitable toys should look, the group around the first Waldorf school started making them for the kindergartens and homes. They taught the schoolchildren how to make them in sewing classes.

The way in which the head is bound off is what especially characterizes this type of doll. The body can vary and has been made differently by different doll makers.

In most Waldorf schools the children made dolls stuffed with wool. It's a wonderful act to make an image of a human being.

The doll—a human image

There are doll collectors throughout the world who fill their homes and whole museums with dolls of all forms and shapes. There the dolls sit and sadly look down at the visitors. Not even in secret do children come and take them down from the shelves and give them life for a few moments! (Or maybe the collector and museum director do it in great secrecy after the visitor has left?)

People who become doll collectors are often the ones who didn't play with dolls as children. They can hide their pent-up desire to play with dolls behind the accepted mask of being a Collector.

But imagine all the dolls that don't get played with!

The doll is special among toys because it is an image of the human being. With the doll's help we can seek our own identity. We can reveal our innermost thoughts, sorrows, and joys to our doll-friend. With the doll's help we can dream ourselves away from a hard reality or prepare ourselves for

younger siblings. So many wonderful and fun things can happen together with the doll.

In German, the word for doll is the same as for pupa. What a wonderful symbolism that every doll is a pupa!— out of which a butterfly can arise, if we only give soul to the doll, give it life.

There are children who see the butterfly in every pupa. They feel for all little animals and dolls and can't do without any of them. Others decide for one doll, and then keep it as their most beloved toy throughout childhood.

It's important that parents treat the dolls with the same respect with which they treat real people. That's why it's so wrong to let children get sloppy dolls that they can hit and box when they feel angry. If the doll is an image of the human being, it must get the same tender care as the children; otherwise it's easy to suspect that you can hit human beings, too.

In Swedish, the word "docka" (doll) means wound-up yarn. In the second half of this book we will learn how to make simple yarn dolls.

Making the doll soft and simple with only dots for eyes and mouth gives the child the freedom to add what is missing.

The stereotyped smile of a plastic doll imposes itself on the child and generates an artificial mood. The cloth doll, on the other hand, changes its expressions according to the mood of the child. It could even be converted to being a boy after first having been a girl (which certainly is unusual)! It doesn't offer the same physical resistance as a corresponding change would meet with from a naturalistic plastic girl. The cloth doll is shaped by the play.

If the child misses a nose on the doll, we can just add one more dot. If the child wonders why the doll has no fingers, we can suggest them with a few stitches.

The cloth doll also doesn't have any interesting mechanism inside it that makes it say "Mama, I want the bottle!" at the most unexpected moments. A technical voice that repeats certain phrases in a monotone awakens the child's curiosity: what's in there that sounds like that? Finally, the child can't resist the urge to take the doll apart and explore its contents.

I clearly remember the strange, slightly aggressive feelings that arose in me because of the rubber stopper my baby doll had on its behind. That it was there so that the doll could be emptied of bath water didn't soften my anger—for me the stopper was a defect that marred my doll. I could never forgive the manufacturer. I also didn't feel good about the text imprinted on the doll's back—I can still feel how my own back itches right there.

Children are strongly influenced by their dearest toys. Let us therefore make them sound and happy.

The infant

Environment: part of the child's inner life

For the little newborn child, life appears dreamlike. It
rests in our arms with total faith and lacks every possibility
of protecting itself. It receives our care and our warmth.

Only when it is warm and feeling well does it reach out
with its eyes. It seems to wonder, To where have I come?
It lies quietly and breathes in the room's atmosphere. Colors,
lights, sounds, movements, and smells as much as food
make up the nourishment for the infant. The infant absorbs
everything; it has no clear borders for what is outside and
inside its own body. The state of being of the people around
the child—which includes their thoughts and feelings—pene-
trates and forms the infant.

Sharp noise or sudden cooling frightens the child and makes
the blood vessels in its body constrict. The infant must then
use all its energy to raise the body temperature again, and
it can't get interested in outside events until the sense of
well-being is restored. All sudden impressions retard the
infant's initial groping attempts to explore the world.

So, if we want to help the infant to feel good we need to
protect it from overly strong impressions. We surround the
cradle with a pastel cloth and make sure that the nursery is
always peaceful.

The fact that the same things are repeated every day in a
certain order helps to reveal a pattern, and the infant slowly
starts to recognize itself. During the first few months, the
daily care, the meetings with the mother or nanny, the impressions from the different rooms, and the excursions out-

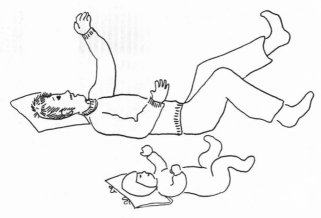

side are more than enough for the infant to get used to.

See for yourself how it is to lie on your back on the floor without being able to turn over onto your stomach. Wave your arms and legs around a little; turn your head from side to side. Pretend that you don't know what anything is. Try to see furniture, curtains, and lamps only as color spots and shapes without depth.

What an amazing place you've ended up in! Sometimes the spot on the ceiling lights up; sometimes it's dark. But you don't have the sharp adult intellect to think about things; you are just there on the floor, and the impressions flow over you.

Human contact vs. material stimulus

If we don't want to or can't carry the infant around with us during our activities in the home (as is done in many other cultures), we can use a basket on wheels as a day bed for the baby who starts to be more and more awake and lies there following our movements with its eyes.

It's important not to use the nightly sleeping place as a safe place to leave the baby during the day, for then it will soon associate the crib with loneliness and disappointment.

In the beginning a baby carriage can be used as a cradle

on wheels for waking hours. Only when the baby seems tired is it put into the crib. Then the baby has two different environments to get to know—which is considerably more exciting than having someone put a red plastic rod with strange things hanging down right in front of your nose when it's supposed that you're bored.

Imagine to yourself how it would feel: you are lying in your bed. You can't move anything more than your head and your arms. You can't talk. You desperately long to be close to some soft, warm, familiar person. You call out. Oh, how wonderful, someone is coming, it's her! But, oh no, she left again. And above your bed, right in the center of attention, she hung up a huge, bright red, arm-thick, plastic rod. On it there is a mirror. You poke the mirror; it swings around, and sometimes you see a sad face in it. It makes you even sadder to see the sad face. You want to be close to a human being, but you have to comfort yourself with a red plastic rod. You are sad, but you're supposed to be happy by looking at a sad face. You are disappointed.

Imagine if you could have lain in a rolling bed in the same room with her and seen what she did instead.

These kinds of so-called educational toys for infants are totally unnecessary, and, to my mind, also damaging. Some children get to have this red rod in their view throughout the whole of their infancy. Before it's over, they've gotten images of even the tiniest parts of their bodies. They can't weed things out; they swallow everything and they are shaped and influenced by everything.

Seeing a little child sit and play with its own mirror-image, I can't help but think of a canary bird chattering at his "lover" in the mirror.

Young children shouldn't be made aware of how they themselves look. But nowadays, wall mirrors—supposedly so good for the infant's self-identification—are installed in day-care centers.

If the baby actually starts believing that it is itself that it sees in that mirror, it only gets confused: but I'm here—I can't be there, too?

When the child has gotten used to mirrors, it starts making

faces and being coquettish in front of them. Isn't it pretty unbearable when young children are affected and self-conscious? They look at themselves with others' eyes, change their voices, and lose their pureness and their spontaneity. To be able to find their own identities they don't need mirrors, but people to meet.

Doesn't it seem exaggerated that infants would need specially contrived toys to be able to develop well? Don't they first of all have to play with their fingers and toes, to try to turn around, feel the sheet and blanket, pull the pajama sleeve, wonder over the fact that the pajamas sometimes change color?

When mother or father picks the baby up, life becomes rich. There's fuzzy hair to pull, a big nose to poke your finger into, a funny round opening full of white, shiny things that opens and closes—little wind puffs come out of it, and a lot of strange, fun sounds. There are two round spots surrounded by tickly hairs and they also can close. And the flying fingers and the hands that can carry, stroke, tickle, clap, and form themselves into almost anything!

Besides that, the mother and father wear clothes that are constantly changing. Buttons, ribbons, necklaces, bracelets, watch. And sometimes another big being shows up with totally new facial features, other smells and sounds.

On the changing-table are usually jars of cream, bottles of oil or powder, and a brush that you can feel.

Only those infants who have to lie in sterile environments without enough human contact are likely to need hang-up toys.

Many people also seem to think that the infant is bored while taking walks. Instead of an enclosed carriage, they buy a panoramic one with a large window in the front so that baby won't miss any of the "stimulating" city traffic. Or they hang up a long string of brightly colored plastic flowers across the baby's line of sight so that it gets absolutely no chance to discover the clouds, the houses, walls, and trees that move by.

But probably the most important thing for the infant is that eye contact is maintained between mother and child, so that the mother's face can calm the child if something frightening happens. The very best arrangement is to carry the infant in a carrier on the mother's front—then mother's voice can also be heard over the traffic noise.

Also, by having a pacifier in its mouth, the child is prevented from getting involved in what is taking place during the walk. It closes itself up and gets a dreamy look. You would do better to save the pacifier for sleeping time.

When the baby can sit up and starts to crawl, it wants to explore, feel, and taste everything. That's when we can put down wooden spoons, jars, boxes, noisy uncolored paper, balls of yarn, balls. We needn't always put out new things; often a familiar object can appear in a new light if it's presented in another room. Or, replace the wooden spoon that the child has been playing with for a long time with another one which is a little different. The child is usually fascinated by the spoon having "changed." But getting only new objects all the time can become tiring for the baby.

When the baby starts crawling around and exploring, we can no longer direct it so easily. There's always a tempting forbidden cord or dangerous piece of furniture. But babies have short memories, and often it's easier than we thought to distract them and carry them into another room where there are some fun shoes with strings or a box with some blocks in it.

With inexhaustible eagerness the child tests how everything tastes, sounds, feels, if you can lift it or pull it. All senses are used.

Summary

The infant cannot protect itself from damaging impressions; it is our task to make the environment calm and secure.

The infant needs no toys; it needs human closeness and warmth. Mirrors only make babies confused or affected. Their best "activity materials" are their own bodies, our hands, faces, hair, and clothes.

Crawling-age babies should be allowed to explore the home in freedom and security.

Toys

Maybe we would still like to give the little baby something? In that case we can make:

- A mobile to hang over the changing-table or bed. Use wooden skewers, thread, and wads of tissue paper of various colors. It will move in the draft and change slowly.

- A knot-doll in a light color, small enough for the baby to lift, can make a fine bed-companion.

- A crocheted rattle. Crochet around and around, making an oblong shape that widens to a ball at the end. Stuff with wool or rags and sew a little bell into the middle of the ball before stitching it all together on the top. Make sure the bell won't be able to come out.

- A soft cloth ball. Cut out four ellipse-shaped pieces of felt. Sew them together, leave one side open, turn and stuff with washed wool fleece, with a ball of yarn, or with cotton rags. Sew up the last side. Make it small enough for the child to hold in one hand.

Gesture (ages 1−2)

The child does what we do

Children who don't have "erect" people around them can't learn how to stand up. In all that they do, children are driven by a strong desire to be like the adults. We do it first and the child does it after. We are happy and the child is content. We worry and the child becomes anxious. We feel joy in working and the children can play.

We do have a great responsibility! We can have all kinds of fancy opinions and theories about how children should be cared for and stimulated, but if we ourselves are nagging and stressed our ideas have no effect. It is our own state of being that the children absorb and imitate.

When the little child stands up and walks, the shoulder area and the arms are freed from the strenuous crawling, the head is held upright, and the child now feels more like us other upright and walking humans. Soon the child starts to use its new ability to reach things that were previously out of reach.

Often the child can walk more easily by holding something in its hand, as if the feeling of "holding on" helps it to balance.

As soon as the gait becomes a little more certain, playfulness appears; the child takes little dance steps and jumps— the joy of being able to follow the parents from room to room!

When we clean the house, Little Sister comes toddling after, carrying all kinds of things. She moves things here and there for reasons unknown to us. Actually, she's doing what we do: she carries things and puts them down again. The purpose of transporting these things she can't comprehend; she's just copying our external gestures.

Little Sister sits and "reads" with little wrinkles on her forehead. She follows seriously and nearsightedly fastens her eyes to the page. After a quick look, she turns the page and stares there. She likes the actual turning of the pages. She's seen on our faces that reading is a serious activity.

By her second birthday, Little Sister has learned a lot about things. She knows that the broom belongs in the corner, that the cup belongs in the kitchen, that the wastebasket is usually under the table, and so on.

The parents proudly brag about Little Sister's neatness. Big Brother is surprised by her willingness to give him his things. But Little Sister is not neat, she just finds joy in the fact that the objects belong in certain places—the confusion of such a multitude of things has started to clear up into an understandable pattern.

As soon as Little Sister gets an idea of where things go, she starts playing with her new knowledge. So she puts her toothbrush among the forks, the shoes in bed, and her pants on her head! She thinks that's really funny and can't understand how we can be so silly as not to be amused.

So many interesting things happen in a home. Inter-esse means to be in-between. That's just what the little child wants. It wants to stick its head up between me and what I'm working with or on. The most fun of all is to join in my activities and get a little bucket and rag and help me wash the cabinets, or to get a personal little piece of dough when I bake. It's not at all as fun to bake when I do the dishes, or to draw when I'm sewing. No, if I'm doing dishes, Little Sister wants to do dishes—preferably in the same bucket! And if I sew, she wants a piece of cloth and a thick needle. Perhaps she'll manage to sew on a button?

Once my little two-and-a-half-year-old happened to see me using a red crayon to color the cheeks of a cloth doll. She disappeared into another room, and all was quiet. After a little while, she was moaning about something and sounded full of pity. I went into her room to see what was wrong. Oh! All the dolls had scarlet fever: they were bright red with the darkest red of the wax crayons all over their faces! Fortunately, wax crayoning wears off textiles fairly quickly.

The child does as the adults do. The precision with which he or she can assume a typical trait from one of the parents or notice how we move around is uncanny.

If I myself have a sagging posture, I can't complain about the child's poor posture.

If I toss toys and dolls all together in a jumble in a box when I clean up, I can't be surprised if the child handles the toys roughly.

If I make dog's-ears and pencil marks in books, I can be sure that the child will also—even if the child's markings will be a little livelier.

The child does like we do, because it loves us and wants to be like us.

Another reason why the little child doesn't want to let the loved ones out of sight is that it's not sure whether or not they're really there when it doesn't see them. That's why peek-a-boo is such a popular game. We hide ourselves for a moment and appear again. The reunion is joyful. From this game the child learns that we come back.

But real hide-and-seek is too scary when you're little. The older children hide themselves so well that you start getting anxious that they're gone for good. The little one wants the one who's hiding to be in the same hiding place each time, so that it can decide for itself how long the uncertainty should last. So, instead of calling the game hide-and-seek, the little one would rather think of it as hide-and-find!

Anna draws

Anna has gotten hold of a crayon. She is one-and-a-half
years old. She has noticed that something shows up when you
move the crayon over a surface. In the beginning she can't
understand the idea of using only paper to draw on; that we'll
have to teach her.

Now she has a sturdy crayon and a large paper. First she
lightly whips her hand around and stares with surprise at the
result. Then she becomes bolder and moves her hand in wide
curves over the paper. The tempo is increased; she becomes
more intense and presses down harder. Her hand moves in
big figure eights and crosses back and forth, layer upon layer.
Sometimes there are whirls that never end. Anna is very
amused and wants to draw often after that.

Let her have thick crayons—for instance, block crayons
that don't break.

If she draws with a lead pencil or ballpoint pen, the results
are pretty pathetic.

Look at her scribbles: there are forms that resemble the
way the child would run through the room—a dance across
the paper instead of on the floor. They can also resemble
whirls of water, planet paths, wind, or plant shapes. Perhaps
the child "knows" more about such things than we suspect.

Anna doesn't need watercolor paint until she understands
the sequence: dip into water, dip into paint, paint. This
understanding comes hardly before the age of three, and
then initially with only one color at a time. Use real watercolors and let her paint on moistened paper so that the paint
flows and shines—large paintbrush!

I feel that smearing finger paint around is an unworthy way
of using paints. Color is, like pure light, ethereal and intan-
gible. Light and color are for the enjoyment of the eye; why
confuse them with mud pies?

The colors of the toys

There is cadmium in Lego pieces; there is lead in the surface paint of smurfs—what are we giving our children?

We can't be telling ourselves that children's need of color is more important than their health? What crass sales motives rule the toy trade? That children love strong colors is an opinion which is widely spread. In modern daycare centers, bold patterns and striking colors are displayed everywhere. Nowhere is there a calm surface!

But color and light are nourishment for us; we are affected by them down into our smallest body cell. There is no doubt that we are affected by spending so much time in artificial light.

We use colors to express moods of the soul; we feel differently in a yellow room than in a red one. "He was in a black mood, she was green with envy, he saw red in anger," etc.

That the eye can apprehend a color is fantastic. It is an ability that we have, and like all abilities it can be developed or dulled. For the eye to meet light, transparent colors is better training than for it to meet smooth, strong, solid colors.

The whole spectrum of colors is present in daylight. Our eye "knows" this. The eye "adds" those colors of the spectrum that are missing when we look at something.

Try for yourself: hold up a plain blue piece of paper against a white background and stare intensely at the blue for a few minutes. Then move your eyes to the white right next to it. Now you see an afterimage on the white— an orange spot. Orange is the complementary color to blue!

In the color circle you see the three primary colors: red, yellow, and blue. Opposite them are their complementary colors: green, purple, and orange. Through mixing the three primary colors, you can get all other colors. Red and yellow give orange, red and blue make purple, yellow and blue make green. Brown and grey come out when all three are mixed.

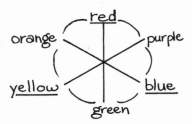

Color circle
The primary colors are underlined.
The complementary colors are
opposite each other.
Two primary colors give a
combination color which is a
complement to the remaining primary
color.

So when you have looked at one of the primary colors—blue, for example—your mind generates the other two primary colors (red and yellow), and you experience the mixture of them—orange!

If you looked at an orange piece of paper the afterimage would be blue.

For every color we see, a complementary color is generated within us so that the three primary colors are always represented.

Children can experience this phenomenon very vividly within themselves. So the colors of the favorite toys and the beloved doll can be important.

You can emphasize a color's character of being light by making it clear and transparent. If you use transparent colors when you paint the children's room, the color won't feel constrictive and lifeless. The material underneath shines through, and nuances that are stimulating to the imagination appear on the surface.

Haven't we all at some time reclined and looked at a spot in the wallpaper and made it turn into all kinds of things, or noticed faces or animals in wood-grain?

Toys can also be glazed so that we can keep in touch with the material of which they are made. Every type of wood has its own structure. This is lost if we pour on plastic color without consideration.

Materials of which the toys are made

Anna is two. She's about to go on an excursion and tests to see if she can lift all the big things that she sees. She puffs

and feels very strong when she manages to lift the big blocks
or daddy's briefcase.

Anna is learning to judge the weight of the materials from
their volume, shape, and material. She's involved in a learning process that takes many years. Even as an adult, Anna
will misjudge and be fooled by a trick.

If we want to help Anna, we don't give her misleading
"information." But we actually do! Just look at the big plastic
block—it looks much heavier than it is. Or take the plastic
doll—what an empty shell! The old rubber dolls at least had
both weight and a certain softness.

That the doll is both heavy and soft and that it feels warm
when you hold it in your arms makes it easier for doll mother
to relate to it, to live in or through it. She receives something back from the doll. It feels good in the bed.

To make the doll that nice to hold, stuff it with washed
wool fleece. Wool fleece stores heat and is not dangerous
for the child if the doll breaks. It is heavier than a stuffing
of synthetic batting or rubber foam, and it's not as flammable.
Wool is a living, natural material.

Wool is also the best material to use for the doll's skin, as
it's soft and warm and resists dirt. But unfortunately, it's
expensive and frequently can't be found in skin colors. So we
often have to settle for cotton instead.

A nice connection between the "dollmaker" and the child is
created if the child gets to see the doll develop, or if it knows
the person who made the doll. Wool and cotton fabric are

such simple materials that the child doesn't need to wonder about what is inside the doll and start taking it apart.

Children learn much from their fingers. They feel different surfaces and structures and often like to have something soft in their hands when they are going to sleep. If the doll feels like the car, the boat, and the blocks, the child is robbed of a lot of experiences. Children who only have plastic toys live in an impoverished environment! In addition, plastic—unlike wood, glass, and metal—has no tone: it sounds totally dead when struck.

Wooden blocks don't lie. They are as heavy as they look, and they are also formable. The wooden car can be fixed and painted. We can have it for many years and really get to know it.

Wooden toys can be made in limited numbers with great variations. Plastic toys, on the other hand, have to be mass-produced because of the expensive machinery involved in making them.

Young children who get to watch TV are prevented by doing so from making their own discoveries about the things and people around them. No matter how good the programs are, insofar as they keep the child away from life they have no value for development.

For young children it's good when things are simple and easy to grasp. Children are fascinated by how a simple shape can have endless variations. Even the most blasé city child collects pine cones, sticks, chestnuts, acorns, and pebbles with touching devotion.

Lego pieces are all steeped in the same form. They don't have the living variety of chestnuts. But nowadays there are so many Lego variations—must it not stimulate the imagination? Yes, they do inspire building. But everything is built on the Lego's conditions.

Look at Anna when she builds with Lego: she knows that as soon as it snaps they're put together. So she builds quickly, and, in a sense, carelessly. Her hand repeats the same motion again and again. Anna doesn't have to consider whether this piece can attach to that one once she's learned to recognize the two of them. She is "locked-in" to the understanding that the piece can be pressed down this way or that. And she knows it'll fall off if she tries to put it on upside down or on its side.

Now watch Anna when she's building with irregular scraps from a carpentry shop. Every piece is different from the other. Before she even attempts to include it with the others, Anna has to weigh each piece in her hand, look at it, and coordinate the facts that her hand and her eye give her. She has to subconsciously make an evaluation: Where can I put this piece so it doesn't fall off? Then she has to place the piece with a light hand and adjust it so that it won't slide off.

The irregular wooden pieces give Anna richer experiences than the Lego. They can also be reshaped, nailed together, painted—and if you tire of them, they can be burned up!

One could say that the Lego needs less manual dexterity than the wooden pieces. And also, a more versatile imagination is needed to create something out of various pieces of wood and other scraps than to put together Lego pieces.

So, if the child does nothing but construct with Lego pieces all day, there is reason to ask if other play materials couldn't be found that would allow more aspects of the child to develop.

The four elements

The four elements, the sun, the moon, and the stars are, like the changes of the seasons, inexhaustible sources for activity in the preschool.

We can blow light feathers and wads of cotton over the table. We can fly kites on windy days. We can fold paper swallows and make streamers that flutter or pinwheels that whirl, and we can chase snowflakes and wilted leaves that come floating down.

We can roast apples, potatoes, and chestnuts. We feed the fire with wood that we have sawn up and carried in; we fantasize about what is concealed in the embers. We find joy in the warmth and cook over the fire.

On the beach in the summer we can dig canals, fetch water in pails, or transform a sandbox into an island world. In spring creeks we can make waterwheels. And indoors we can play in the bathtub with mugs, funnels, and gurgling water.

Children usually manage to find the last unpaved piece of earth that's left, wherever they live. And especially after a rain it's wonderful to squish your feet into the mud. The garden plot is a wonderful place for digging and searching for worms and little crawling things.

Fantasizing about the moon and the stars is exciting, and so is observing a real glowing sunset.

There are songs and stories that are about the beings in the wind and the air, about the heat of the fire, about boats on the ocean, and about the mole in the earth. (And if we don't know of any, we can make them up!)

Don't take away the child's spontaneous joy and immediate experience of all that nature has to offer. Don't start explaining for the child how rain is created and how snowflakes are made—don't destroy the child's wonder when a snowflake has gotten stuck on its coat and lies there gleaming white like a magic flower. Don't drag in the encyclopedia's boring explanation of how crystals appear!

Let preschool children retain their wonderful images, for these images are real and true for them. The child will "sober up" in time and will want to learn how it "really" is. Give the child "images"—not numbers and scientific terminology. When the child asks "How strong is the wind?" don't answer that it's half-gale and is blowing at about seventeen meters per second (thirty-eight miles per hour). Answer that the wind is so strong it can carry the leaves and even knock over trees sometimes.

Summary

Young children need to see adults who are engaged in visible, practical jobs around them.

The youngest children move around after us and imitate our gestures, often without understanding the purpose of our actions.

Scribbles are the child's movement put on paper.

Color is light and light is for us a nourishment without which we can't feel well. Treat color with respect; paint in subtle nuances to develop the receptivity of the eyes.

Natural, simple, graspable materials are best for the preschool child. Don't fool little Anna by giving her objects that "lie." A block that looks heavy should also be heavy.

Give the child toys that it can understand how they are made, or better yet, that it has participated in making.

The "four elements," air, fire, water, and earth make fine playmates!

Let the child live with you—it learns in freedom without pedagogical admonitions, explanations, or information!

Toys (ages 1–2)

Suggestions:

- Knot-doll.
- Large sack doll or coverall doll.

- Doll bed made of a cardboard box or a wooden cradle, pillow, blanket, and mattress.
- Doll carriage that can be pushed and that won't easily tip over.
- Large, soft ball to throw with both hands.
- Play blanket to hide under.
- Large basket, or drawer to keep their things in.
- Irregular blocks, scraps from a carpentry shop. (Older children can file off, sand, and paint them with watercolor and a fixing agent, or oil them with linseed oil plus petroleum spirits, and give them away as presents.)
- A movable toy—for example, a duck that waddles when pulled.
- Rocking chair, or the like.

Outdoors: pail, shovel, ball, and all that nature offers!

Language (ages 3—4)

Rhymes and verses

The child eventually learns to control more and more difficult body-movements. It tries to fly and is surprised that it
keeps falling down again. It does somersaults, tries to stand
on its head, rolls down the grassy slope on its side, twirls
around in the swing.

In pace with this physical development, language flourishes.
The first laboriously expressed words were about simulta-
neous with the first tottering steps. Now that the child can
run and jump, it starts to rhyme, sing, and rattle off verses.
The language has limits; it must be explored! If you babble
you sometimes get real words, sometimes not. Children
practice intonation and single sounds.

As he or she "tasted" furniture, clothes, food, and toys
during crawling age, the child is now tasting the sounds of
the language.

Now it's a question of feeding the child with funny words!
Most of us have access to words, these cheapest of our toys.

But don't fall into talking baby-language to the child just
because the child sounds so cute when it pronounces the
words. The child can feel offended if we meet it at a level
which is far below our own.

The three-year-old's eyes shine as he gets to ride our
knees to the rhythm of "Ride a Cock Horse to Banbury Cross."

We adults can often feel that the contents of the old rhymes
and songs are quite strange or even reactionary, but the children care more about the rhythm and the rhyme than about
the contents. They are captivated by all happy verses and

quickly learn them by heart.

The otherwise so difficult way home from nursery school is made shorter if we make up a rhyme about things we see. If the child is forced to think backwards in time and answer all the questions about what happened during the day, or if it has to think ahead and plan the dinner with us, the walk home becomes heavy and tiresome.

Here we are walking right now, thinks the child.

The doll, the child's alter ego

The child gets practice in expressing feelings and experiences during play with dolls. It meets itself in the doll. The child gives the doll life, ensouls it with his or her imagination.

Usually the first play with dolls starts early; even the one-year-old bends down over the doll carriage and kisses the doll.

The two-year-old lifts the doll with a sturdy grip around some part of the doll—where isn't so important.

If it's time for the doll to sleep, it's pushed down into the carriage again and gets a blanket forcefully pressed down

around its sides.

A little while later it's time for the doll to get up again: the blanket is taken off and the doll is pulled up, given an impulsive hug, and dragged along on an expedition. It can end up being in either water puddles or the bathtub, in the dirt in the yard, or furthest-in under a chest. Sometimes it's realistically fed with yogurt and other times it's totally forgotten.

Many children don't care about dressing and undressing the doll, but they want it to come along as a friend on all adventures. A doll with attached clothes—like the "coverall doll" Christopher, see photo next page—is good for them.

Andy is four years old and has just gotten a big dress-up doll with pajamas just like his own. He looks lovingly at the doll and tucks it in next to him every night. He has a friend. They are going to have a lot of fun together.

When Andy gets older, he makes a parachute for the doll and lets it out of an upstairs window. In the Indian-books age, the doll gets its own Indian outfit, naturally. When Andy is sick, or when he goes traveling, the doll always comes along.

Andy, four years old, has a cold and is tired of it. He regards his doll intently, suddenly lights up and says:

"Mommy, lucky doll who doesn't have a nose—then he can't get a stuffy nose!"

In the rhymes-and-verses age, the dolls often get strange names: Curly-Burly, Workerman Doll, Mushi, Margerini.

Sometimes the doll is given the child's own name: then it really is the child's alter ego.

True-to-life toys

Perhaps Andy also wants a soft animal. But don't give him one that looks like a caricature of a human being.

Try to find animals that really look like animals, without being too detailed and realistic. The best toys are those that show the distinctive feature of whatever they represent—for example, a wooden animal that captures a typical movement which shows just that animal's particular bearing.

If we give young children caricatures and comic figures to play with, we assume that they have an ability which they really don't—the ability to see that a caricature is amusing.

To be able to caricature a person, you have to know what a person really looks like. But young children don't know that! Just look at their own pictures of people: not many details are included.

Young children can't critically observe what is typical for a face. And we shouldn't teach them how to, because that will awaken too early a consciousness which belongs to later ages.

There are puzzles on blocks for young children where you see a face pictured so that the nose is on one block, the mouth and chin on another, and the eyes on a third.

It is foreign for young children to divide a wholeness in such an abstract way. It almost hurts them to cut up a face into different pieces. It's just as unpleasant for them to lift away a piece of the man's stomach, half of the cat's ear, etc., in a large puzzle. Better for young children are those puzzles with sawed-out whole figures that can be played with

---

Christopher is a doll 25 cm. (just under 10 in.) tall with an attached knitted blue coverall. The way we play as children reveals how we will work as adults: quickly or slowly, concentratedly or distractedly.

when taken out.

Much of what is painted for young children has thick black outlines, as if the manufacturer thought that the children can't see well unless the men's boundaries are strongly marked. But those strong black lines don't exist in reality!

Two surfaces aren't demarcated by lines. They are just next to each other. My pink hand on the table isn't surrounded by anything black; it's pink, and where it ends the brown table takes over!

Andy draws

The generous curves and spirals that filled the paper earlier now clear up into single crosses and circles.

Andy is now three years old, and he is struggling to draw a round ring. He holds his breath with effort and sighs with relief when he finally manages.

The ring is a symbol for unity, wholeness; it is a closed room. Andy has started to experience the fact that there is an outside and an inside of him. He is the circle. He now says "I" about himself in full consciousness. He will have his earliest childhood memories from this period.

Out of the round ring the head-legs man appears. Arms and legs grow right out of the head.

Is it possible that Andy's circle moves in another direction than Daddy's? Andy tests how his own ego relates to others' egos. He wants and he does not want (which we call "obstinacy").

Now Andy needs to know where the limits are: this is what we do and this is what we don't do. Then he feels secure. But in Barbapapa's amoeba-like world, where everything is possible, Andy doesn't feel particularly comfortable. There his round ring is totally without stability; it slackens and sways!

Andy, four years old, wants to draw. He doesn't hesitate, just starts right ahead! And then something appears which gives him an idea of how he's going to continue. While he draws, he describes what he sees with amazement—as if it were someone else that was drawing:

"This seems to be a boat that's bobbing—and oh, it's so spotted! Does it have the measles? And I see it's really windy, because the flag is flapping. But what's swimming under the boat? A dangerous fish!"

With delight he shows Daddy what he's made. When Daddy picks up the picture later in the day and looks at it, Andy comes and tells him proudly that the picture represents something totally different than before: a map, rain, cliffs.

"What?" says Daddy, but manages to stop what he was about to say: "But this morning you said it was a boat and a fish!"

It simply isn't a boat any more for Andy. He now sees totally different things in the picture.

Change, transform!

During play these kind of changes occur all the time. A few

four- and five-year-olds don't need much to create major dramas. With short orders from the oldest, the parts are distributed:

"Let's say that you're the mother and I'm the father, and you get to be our little baby, and you can be the dog."

And it's started. If playmates are lacking, the dolls will do.

Now you better keep up, for childbirths, generation changes, and role changes can happen very fast in this age group.

"Now you were born, now you could crawl—no let's say you could walk—now you're coming with me when I go shopping."

The children look around the room, and everything they see is usable. The sofa is a boat one moment, and the next moment it's a house with a blanket for a roof. Children in this age group let the impressions from the things around them strongly influence their playing.

The way that children combine words, objects, and experiences into an unconventional "jumble" during play can be compared with how we adults let our thoughts associate freely in our dreams.

Children take of what is served and happily blend in their own memories, the whim of the moment, visual impressions, the room's furniture, unexpressed needs, experiences of their own bodies, sounds, what mommy just said....

The child creates a wonderful collage out of everything that is in and around it at that moment. While the playing continues, the child tests all kinds of words and sounds to see if they are usable and if the other children will understand.

It's actually damaging for a child to one-sidedly strain certain muscles for long periods. To demand, for example, that he or she should follow my monotonous pace during a walk is to expose a child to a form of overexertion. Another form of overexertion is to have the child sit and put little beads into a frame for an hour.

No, the child wants life and movement. And it certainly isn't a sign of lack of concentration if the child often switches from activity to activity. Children are sanguine beings. They want to fly from flower to flower to see what is offered, just like a butterfly. Then, after a while, they like to get back to the first flower again.

That television offers variety is something that we only imagine. In actual fact, the child is forced to sit still unreasonably long. The muscles of the eye are held at a constant position, as the distance to the TV image is always the same. The TV image doesn't have depth like a mirror does.

Repetition

Just because children like movement and change so much doesn't mean that they would be happy if everything always changed and was never the same. On the contrary, they like to hear the same story again and again. They know if the words aren't the same at each occasion. The known pattern gives them delight and security. The child knows the story and "dares" to be frightened by the scary giants and trolls. An unknown story with an unknown outcome can get too scary!

Young children appreciate simple funny stories and verses, for example, The House That Jack Built, The Pancake, The Seven Little Kids, the song about Little Briar Rose, Ring Around a Rosie, Goldilocks, The Three Little Pigs, and so on.

If we ourselves can only overcome our resistance to repeating the same words, we'll notice how the children absorb and enjoy the limited supply of words. It's the words' relation to each other—the rhythm and the melody—that they grasp and then use in their play.

A little verse read every night becomes a secure entrance into the world of sleep. Even we adults generally have some rituals that we always perform before we go to bed.

If weekdays are given a certain rhythm and weekends another, the child soon starts to experience that there is a rhythm of the week.

If we repeat an act many times, we get a more balanced view of it.

If we go for a walk in a certain forest grove every Sunday, more and more details eventually appear—strange little creatures that we didn't see the first times, remarkable flowers, crooked branches, beautiful stones, the chirping of birds, and the rustle of mice.

If we tell a story many times, we perceive more little details than if we hear it only once and then immediately hear another.

A little Christmas play with simple dolls can appear to be new every year. The children have changed during the year, and they therefore see the play with new eyes.

The zoo and the ant

We are so anxious to show our children reality. We go sight-seeing in life with them, drag them to museums and to zoos to entertain and inform them. At the zoo, we rush

impatiently ahead without taking the time to wait until the squirrel comes to our hand or the sparrow sits on our shoulder.

We call "come along, hurry up now, otherwise we won't have time to see the bears, too!" to the child who is absorbed in watching a little ant walk across the path. Then when we come home, exhausted after several hours of trudging at the zoo, we discover to our exasperation that the three-year-old's greatest retained pleasure from the excursion was—the little ant!

Do you have to go to the zoo to look at ants?

Summary

The child gradually plays itself into its body, and at the same time conquers the language.

Rhymes and verses are nourishment for the child and further imagination and language development.

Let the preschool child live in the here and now.

Young children don't understand caricatures. Give them "real" animals that show each animal's distinctive feature without thereby being too realistic.

Spare Andy from puzzles where people have been sawn into random pieces!

The three-to-four-year-old plays games of transformation and gets inspiration from the outside.

Any one-sided training overexerts the child. Let it alternate between activity and movement.

Repetition gives security. The same good-night verse every night facilitates falling asleep. To hear the same song many times makes us more sensitive to its slightest changes.

First take possession of the little world, the home, the neighborhood; then take excursions further and further away.

First the ant—then the zoo!

Toys (ages 3—4)

Children don't need much to be able to play. Give them scraps from your own activities and let them take part in your activities. Avoid coloring books where children are urged to fill in ready-made black contours.

Some suggestions:

- Knot-doll.
- Large, simple doll.
- A few clothes for the doll that are easy to put on and take off.
- A doll bed made of cardboard, a wooden cradle, doll carriage, or sleeping bag.
- Mattress, pillow, blanket, sheet when the child first manages to make the bed with them.
- Various pieces of cloth to sew with or to wrap the baby in.
- Some large cloths in cheerful colors for making houses or dressing up with.
- A funny hat, an old purse, some pieces of jewelry.
- Gold paper, tissue paper, crepe paper, nontoxic glue.
- Block crayons, wax crayons, and thick large sheets of paper.
- Large wooden truck with a platform, a few smaller cars.
- Wooden pieces of various shapes for building.
- A few simple animals.
- Moving toys: jumping jack, hens that peck, old men that saw.
- Little baskets or boxes for collecting pretty stones and other things.
- A rocking horse.
- A table which, when put on its side, can be transformed with the help of some blankets into a store, house, car, etc.

Outdoors: bucket, shovel, rake, forms, ball, wheelbarrow, pinwheel, bark boats, swing, etc.

Thought (ages 5—6)

Inner conceptions

The five-year-old is generally calm and quite happy with himself. He can actually be quiet for long periods! He gives an impression of greater purposefulness and composure. He has matured to the extent that he can find words to express his disappointments instead of rolling on the floor and kicking. He starts "philosophizing."

All the great questions of life are typical for the five-year-old. Who are we human beings, anyway?

"Mommy, what do you think is the best on people?" my five-year-old asked very seriously. After having politely listened to my answer he said,

"I think the best on people are their hands—and arms." (We can see the importance that children give hands in the fact that they are drawn quite large in children's drawings.)

Another day he said:

"Isn't it strange that we can see something inside our head, even if it isn't here!"

He had discovered that we have inner conceptions.

On the ice-skating rink he pondered over why the long-distance skaters who made such slow leg-movements nonetheless made faster progress than the ice-hockey players who moved their legs so quickly!

"Where did I come from?" asks the five-year-old. "Who made everything in the whole world?"

But the child is not asking for a lecture on sexuality or about gas nebulae. The child asks:

"Where was I when you were small?"

Preferably, he then wants to hear that he was somewhere. The thought "you didn't exist" is too incomprehensible, and it hurts to hear that "when you die you don't exist any more." It feels better to hear some indication that "before you came to us you were somewhere, and you looked at all the people, and you chose a mommy and daddy and came to us." It's nice for me as a parent to imagine that my children have chosen just me and nobody else to come to; therefore I must make an effort to show them that they made a good choice.)

When the children ask questions, we must listen intently. How much do they want to know? We strengthen their ability to form concepts if we give them imagelike descriptions that they can enter into with their imagination. Photographs of cosmos and childbirth, on the other hand, limit and inhibit this ability.

The five-year-old usually shows a great interest in letters. This interest often subsides in the six-year-old, who would rather devote itself to physical activities and who is a little messy in a general sense. Then the interest reappears in the seven-year-old child.

A five-year-old who spends a lot of time reading is prevented by doing so from making firsthand experiences. The letters, like the television, can fascinate the child so that it is kept still longer than it actually wants to be. Afterwards there is a fatigue reaction in the form of noisy overactivity.

Letters are too abstract, too dead, to be good stimulation for younger children. We can't prevent a child from learning to read early, but we can keep it from being bent over magazines and books for hours. The child should get to hear many stories and be given many opportunities for active play with other children.

The child asks questions, but does best with suggestive, imagelike answers from us. If the child asks what the stomach looks like, then vividly describe the large sack where all the food goes! But don't show a TV program or a book where the human being is taken apart into his individual parts, organs, blood circulation, muscles, etc. Then the child just starts to hurt everywhere and starts to worry that the different parts won't hold together properly. Then the child turns into a little hypochondriac. Let the child's imagination take hold of living images and then form its own conceptions. Later, way up into school age, the child will be mature enough to see detailed charts of his own insides. The child will then like to keep a distance from things, to get an overview, to be critical.

While playing, children in this age group get their inspiration from within themselves. The child now has clearer ideas about what it wants to enact than it did earlier. Outer circumstances aren't allowed to influence the playing as much as before. The child sees the whole of its play within itself.

Listen to a few children of that age as they play. First they sketch a framework for the play, and then they speak in the past tense:

"Let's say you were a man who came to visit, and I was a mommy who was going out with her baby, and you had a high hat."

When all important facts are established the child says:

"Now we'll begin," and they thereby start talking in the present tense.

"Knock, knock, says the man, knock, now I'm going in— Hello, isn't the daddy home today?"

"No, he's out right now."

"Oh, that's too bad."

Now the actors stop themselves; they notice that the hat is missing. The man was supposed to have a high hat. They rush to the dress-up basket and get a hat:

"This can be the hat."

Then, feeling that their playing now corresponds to their inner image of how it was supposed to be, they theatrically repeat the whole beginning.

The playing now has a special mood. Whereas during younger years the borders between playing and other activities were quite loosely defined, now the children can suddenly stop playing. Conflicts often arise because the children have different ideas of how it should be:

"No, let's play something else now." Or:

"If you won't do like I want you to, I'm not going to play!"

They can withdraw from the play when it doesn't suit them any more.

Maria draws

Children reveal many things in their drawing that they can't yet express in words.

If we can interpret their motives, it's sometimes possible to help them manage something that's worrying them. But it easily happens that our too-obvious interest in their pictures can make them self-conscious and result in their no longer being able to create spontaneously.

If we excitedly throw ourselves all over everything Maria draws and immediately hang it up on the walls, Maria soon starts to produce for our sake!

It's not the result, the finished drawing, that should be admired, but the activity itself. We find joy in the fact that Maria draws, so she fills up the whole paper and uses such happy colors. It's nice to save typical pictures, but do it without a big fuss.

We don't ask the child what everything represents, because then it may feel forced to tell us things that it's really not experiencing. But we listen, of course, when he or she comes to us on their own and tells us what the picture shows.

If we give the child only a few sheets of paper at a time, he or she won't be tempted to be wasteful or sloppy.

Maria is six and wants to draw. She hesitates for a long time with the crayon in her hand: "What should I draw?" Finally she decides: "I'll draw a horse running on a meadow."

Then she starts. The horse is brown, naturally, and the meadow is green. She has become a realist. The four-year-old could happily make a brown sun and a purple lawn, but Maria can be disappointed:

"The yellow crayon is gone—I can't make the sun!"

Maria can also observe her drawing critically and crumple it up, dissatisfied: "It's no good." The picture didn't correspond to her inner idea of how a horse on a meadow looks.

In the same way, a whole play can stop if the children can't find something that can be a cash register when they play store. They walk around looking for an object that will correspond to their idea of a cash register. Perhaps the toy dresser where the drawer can bang shut will do. But the four-year-old would gladly have taken any old block or shoe!

Come and play, Mommy!

If Maria is alone, she'll probably often try to get Mommy or Daddy involved in her playing. The parent is given a role, and Maria watches carefully so that no mistakes are made. You can't fall out of the role for a moment.

Many children can turn this situation into total tyranny. Their poor parents can't ever be themselves. Besides that, the home becomes inhabited by invisible friends on whom you shouldn't sit down by mistake.

Other children tell endless stories about their own secret kingdom. These fantasies are images of what is happening within the child. They should be respected, but without being made the main interest of your time together. In spite of it all, I want to be with the real-life child—not all her invisible friends. (You also have to ask yourself if these daydreams have arisen from a longing for friends or from a feeling of not being loved.)

Parents generally make exaggerated demands on themselves. They think that they have to put on advanced entertainment for at least half an hour as soon as the child asks them to play, so they say no.

Surprisingly little is actually demanded if the children have gotten used to playing by themselves. Mommy can continue sewing and just stick out a foot to get bandaged, and Maria is happy with the hospital play. To let out a dangerous growl as I sit reading can be enough to have Maria totally convinced that I am a wild boar!

My daughter Clara once came in to me as I sat sewing and said to me:

"Mommy! Let's pretend that you were my mommy and I was your daughter!"

Really an inspiring game, I thought. Now I really had to put myself above my adult conventions not to burst out:

"But I am your mommy!"

I really made an effort, and finally managed to catch a glimpse of the exciting possibilities of being another mommy to another child—a totally new situation! I disguised my voice, pulled my glasses down onto the tip of my nose and pretended to be very strict.

Clara was delighted! It was another mother!

The doll friend

Doll merchants' daughters, who had any number of fine dolls to play with, didn't want to have anything to do with dolls—except for the old "smelly" rag doll from grandmother's days!

A six-year-old got a big plastic doll that could talk. It wasn't long before the doll was taken apart and the speech mechanism was taken out. The doll's shell was thrown in a corner, and the speech mechanism was bedded down and cared for with much love!

Most children, however, who get a plastic doll do play with it. They fantasize and talk to the plastic dolls just like they do with the soft dolls or with their other things.

But the plastic doll with its modeled face is often assigned a given role. It is confined to a narrower range within the child's play. The same applies to all toys that have pronounced features. All caricatures play certain roles and can't exchange with one another. Punch, for instance, is Punch, and he can't take over the giant's lines in the Punch and Judy show.

A doll whose features are only suggested gives the child greater freedom during the play.

Terrible tragedies can occur when the favorite doll is lost. It's comparable to losing a close relative. Therefore the child must be allowed to work through the grief and loss and be comforted. Don't give him or her the brisk words:

"But honey, it was just a doll; come on and we'll buy a new one."

We wouldn't say that to a parent who has lost his child. But we can comfort and say:

"Perhaps your doll came to another home where another boy or girl is happy with it, and maybe you will soon find another little friend who will need you."

For some children the doll can never be replaced, but the child could transfer its strong feelings to a living little pet instead. Other children find another doll, totally different from the first, and start to feel connected with it.

Getting a big baby doll is very special for some children, especially if a new sibling has recently arrived in the family. It can be sewn using the largest pattern (D—using double material; see pp. 134, 135), and it can inherit real baby clothes if the sleeves are folded up and the pants shortened.

But it doesn't need real ointment! Most children do just fine with "air-ointment." Any ointment that does get smeared in, however, can be washed out with lukewarm water, soap, and a nailbrush.

We can help the children install a simple doll house in a box or on a bookshelf. Homemade furniture made of little boxes and pieces of wood stimulates the child to make more. You can make the finest little household utensils out of beeswax; the child can draw little paintings for the walls; older children can weave rugs in a weaving frame.

If given a fantastic doll house with lights in all the rooms and a thousand details, the child will very likely sooner or later let the dolls move out of the house with some furniture and move into a strange little corner. It's more challenging

to the imagination to see how you can arrange things temporarily than to play in the ready-made doll house. Fine doll houses are probably expressions of a grown-up's desire to play, but for children they usually end up being curios.

Doll-house dolls can be yarn dolls (for description, see p. 127) or small knot-dolls with clothes. See page 111.

Impressions from the senses

Impress. Something is pressed into me. My senses get an impression. You can hear from the word that we are shaped by what we see, hear, feel, smell, taste, experience.

Sense impressions and our ability to interpret them make it possible for us to orient ourselves in time. Therefore it is important to take care of our senses so that they can function well. Often nowadays our senses are unnecessarily allowed to become dulled.

There are city children who are afraid of the quiet of the night. They don't know what the little noises in the house are, so they are afraid. They jump at a creak from the hallway; they're made anxious by the beating of their own hearts and by the swishing of the blood in their heads. These are sounds that they can't hear during the day because of the traffic noise or the noisy daycare center, or because their parents constantly have the TV or radio on.

The senses need time. If we start with simple and subtle experiences it will be much easier later on for the child to absorb complicated and strong impressions on the basis of this foundation of earlier experiences.

It's nice for children to start with single notes when they listen to music—not with a whole orchestra. A single flute or a few subtle tones from a string instrument may be good. Listening to many songs sung by a live voice—not from a record—

Nini is 30 cm. (nearly 12 in.) tall, has thin pigtails, and is sewn out of a brown cotton sock. The beloved doll friend always listens and is willingly protected by the child.

and to simple pieces from one single instrument is best for the child's hearing.

Even adults can be struck with a kind of "culture shock" if they suddenly enter an environment where everything is foreign and incomprehensible to them. They can become totally apathetic. The child has to be able to recognize himself in order to be able to be receptive to novelty.

The ear has to know what quiet is in order to be able to apprehend the whole range of sounds.

Young children assume the traits of the beloved people around them. There are many examples of children who have gotten crooked backs, who limp, or who show other signs of bodily damage, even though they are found to be totally healthy when examined. They have simply picked up one of the parent's ways of moving.

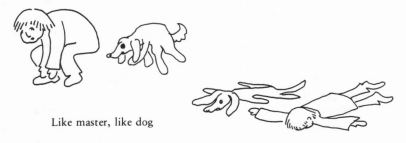

Like master, like dog

Not only people, but beloved toys—especially dolls and soft animals—can influence the child. Objects to which we give loving attention will, of course, make the strongest impressions on us.

Falling asleep with a totally soulless, limp, and loose doll in view, for example, will surely not contribute to giving the child a straight and firm posture. On the other hand, a doll with friendly and healthy looks and a firm, warm body contributes to giving the child stability.

In the same vein, if the child falls asleep after watching TV for an hour or so every night, it is very strongly patterned by the program contents.

Summary

The five/six-year-old is, at least at times, calm and "philosophical."

We help him or her the most if we give only suggestive answers to questions—answers that give their own imaginations room to thrive.

The child now draws much of the inspiration for playing from within its own conceptions. Children usually need less of our own participation than we think to get started with their play.

A doll with features only suggested and a simple doll house favor the imagination. They can be changed endlessly.

Impressions are "pressed in" to the child and shape him. Choose with care what impressions your child will get.

The senses need time to mature. Start with simple and subtle experiences of color, music, dance, etc.

Toys (ages 5—6)

Don't forget to take away toys when the child has too many.

Toy suggestions:

- The child can make its own knot-dolls.
- A dress-up doll with clothes; a baby doll with "diapers" and cradle.
- A whole family of doll-house dolls or yarn dolls.
- A simple doll house in a box or bookcase.
- Homemade doll furniture and utensils.
- Beeswax. You can buy it in cakes; it smells good, has fine colors, and is nontoxic. Warm it in the hands and shape it: when it hardens, it can be played with. Can be re-used forever.
- Pieces of fabric, needle and thread in a little sewing kit.
- Pieces of fabric for playing and dress-up clothes in a bag or suitcase.

- Wax crayons, watercolors, broad paint brushes, large sheets of paper.
- Colored paper to cut; nontoxic glue.
- Wooden scraps, wooden wheels, sticks, hammer and nails. Help to saw! Sandpaper, file, and wood glue.
- Blue clay.
- Cars.
- Soft and hard animals; fence blocks for barn.
- Empty boxes and jars.
- Baskets for little things.
- Swing.
- Movable picture from favorite story.

Outdoors: bucket, shovel, rake, ball, pullcart, wagon, jump rope, marbles, high swing, tops, kites, boats, paper swallows.

The school-age child

The imagination flourishes

Being ready for school entails an incredible transformation. The child kind of stands up tall and looks us in the eye in a different way. Now almost every cell of the body has been changed, the change of teeth has begun—the child has made its "own" body to continue growing in.

Now follows a second seven-year-period, up to puberty, when memory, imagination, and feeling especially dominate the development. Now the curiosity for life outside the home and preschool is aroused. Now the child wants to test its powers and to get to know new authorities. Imagination flourishes, and the child welcomes images from fairytales, fables, legends, and myths.

Never are we likely to be in such perfect control of our body movements as during the years between starting school and entering puberty. See how schoolchildren slide down slides standing up and climb with perfect balance. They play; they are musicians, and their body is the instrument; they are filled with seldom-heard tones.

This is the most "quick-to-learn" age—the devouring age. Children gather data and absorb material for their memories. Many school-age children develop special interests and soon know everything worth knowing about the Amtrak schedule, state birds, or animals threatened by extinction. Some collect stamps; others have secret codes and languages; still others save labels or tickets.

The thorough knowledge is used by the child in its fantasy creations, model-building, drawings, miniature societies.

The child wants to collect, arrange, and get an overview.

During puberty, many of these skills are lost for a period during which the teenager is unhappy with him/herself and everyone else. Then he or she becomes critical and looks at everything from a greater distance. The experience of their own body is in the way. They can't think of anything but themselves and the world situation. It's no longer possible to study with the same concentration.

When the child starts school, it compares itself with other children. The issue is one of melting into the group and matching the pace of others. During recess, for example, children play together according to their own rules, and if someone is late he or she often doesn't get to play: there they are stricter than the teacher.

Only the bravest children can put themselves above the group's decisions. If you're a little shy you don't dare insist on joining in. Adults can help by, once in a while, organizing games where everyone joins in.

When the children discover that they can make rules for the ball game and for hopscotch, they soon make up their own rules of the most varying kinds. You can see schoolchildren in wild fights about whether to do this or to do that is permitted.

Soon they have rules for everything: you have to get on all buses through the wrong door; you have to balance on the edge of the sidewalk and climb a strange roundabout way to school every morning; you have to stake so many marbles in the marble game and say a certain verse when you skip rope; you're popular if you carry swapping-goods and can swap things with the others according to strict market rules. Having learned that there are rules that people have to abide by in order to live with each other, the schoolchildren practice social dynamics in their play.

Johnny draws

During school age, the child's drawings often lose some of the force and boldness that characterized them earlier. Johnny checks to see what the neighbor draws and adapts to certain norms—this is good and that is bad! He makes an effort to draw as well as an older, admired friend. Now he needs much encouragement to dare draw and paint spontaneously.

Johnny can now burst out:

"Oh, look how beautiful!" when he sees a lovely view.

Earlier he saw only that the clouds moved across the sky, or that a car moved in the distance. But now he enjoys the beauty in what he sees, with the consequence of becoming critical towards his own creations. He's started being able to compare them with what others are doing. He tries to draw perspectives.

Johnny can also draw a face and a whole person pretty well. He knows now what a face looks like. Knowing that, he can start to play with his knowledge: he draws caricatures, comic figures.

At around the age of nine, when he has reached the level of linguistic and mental development where he can tell adult jokes and understand the point in them, Johnny draws his own comic strips and magazines.

Doll play during school years

Many children who might not earlier have played much with dolls may now enter a real doll-playing phase. They take the dolls along everywhere; they want things for the doll; they put the doll to bed every night before they themselves go to bed; they sew lots of clothes and tiny belongings for the doll. They let the dolls go on school outings.

In the stores you can buy Barbie, Cindy, Action Man, and all the others—dolls like photo models with skinny legs or "he-man muscles," with eyes like dead fish and sickening vinyl plastic skin. They have thousands of accessories, sport clothes, horses, swimming pools, makeup tables, space equipment, diving clothes, racing cars, and other status symbols. They convey a life-style that is really questionable.

If we want to give the child an alternative to these dolls, we can make the smallest of the dress-up dolls in this book—size A. It will make a small, dainty doll that the child can

A small doll like this (20 cm.—about 8 in.) is suitable for school-age children. They can make clothes themselves for this doll, which is a soft alternative to the stiff, status-seeking Barbie and Action Man.

help to sew. If the doll's hair is made of strong cotton thread, it can be combed and coiffed just fine.

Even those children who consider themselves too old to play with dolls can find much joy in sewing clothes for the little doll and in quietly inventing imaginary adventures for it.

It's not at all embarassing to have a doll sitting on your bed if you've made it yourself—even if you're a tough guy.

Children about ten years old and up can, with some assistance, make all the dolls described in this book.

The large dress-up dolls are the most difficult, especially when it comes to the proportions and the assembly of the different parts. But schoolchildren usually don't hesitate to constantly ask "Is this the right way?" as so many adult doll-makers do.

They just sew and happily tell you that they're "actually not going to bind off the head, it's too much work" or that "it doesn't need feet, does it?"

Tiny dolls can be made in exactly the same way by reducing the pattern in the book, which can make a cute minidoll to have in your pocket.

Parents can often make blunders—don't we remember that from when we were young? Our own children notice it also. We should, for example avoid saying:

"You're so big, you don't have to drag along that dirty old doll all the time!"

Let Johnny himself realize that he's left childhood behind him. If we force him to throw away a beloved old doll, he might lose his trust in us. As long as the doll has a little bit of his soul in it, he can't separate himself from it without pain. One day he himself will notice that the doll is empty, that the butterfly has left its pupa, and then he'll suggest that we give it or put it away.

Meaningful activities

In cultures other than ours the seven-year-old is already incorporated into the adult life. It is given duties according to its abilities to help the family support itself.

For better or for worse, children in developed countries are spared the burden of supporting the family. It's good, of course, that we don't have child labor any more, through which young children were used for hard factory work that ruined them and took away their childhood. But it's bad if children are left out of the adults' "important" activities and are relegated to a "useless" nursery world.

It's not so easy, though, to find suitable activities for the children in our mechanized homes. A lot of practical chores are either transformed into incomprehensible mechanical events or are forbidden because of being dangerous.

So how is Johnny going to grow into our society in a natural way? How is he going to get part of the responsibility for our getting food and a roof over our heads?

I feel that it's an important task for us adults to find chores that Johnny can help with, in spite of all the machines.

We can let him wash fine woolens by hand; we can let him mix dough, whip cream, cut vegetables. He can tell us what we need at the store. He may be able to buy one or two things in the corner grocery store. He can cook the food if we tell him what to do (and don't notice the mistakes).

Some children are realists and happily busy themselves with practical things, perform "assignments" with an important air. Others are imaginative bohemians who do only what they themselves want.

Most children are sensitive to being forced. They can absolutely not understand any "democratic" reasoning of the type: Everyone in the family has to make their beds and you have to do the dishes once a week, because I do. A three-year-old doesn't understand that at all. But it's fun to "help" do the dishes when Mommy's doing them. And out of that joy and habit, Johnny can turn out to be a very helpful eight-year-old.

There is a category of toys which often disappoints children. It includes toy tools, toy instruments, toy pots and pans, toy binoculars, etc. —things that look so realistic that the child is led to believe that they are usable as real things.

But when Johnny goes to saw with the toy saw, it bends and

is hopelessly dull. And the doll saucepan that looked so real smells of burned paint when it's put on the stove.

It's much more fun to get some real tools, saucepans, and musical instruments—not as many tools as the adult, because then there's nothing left to long for, but durable things that work. A little box containing a needle, thread, and scissors, for example, and a few cute pieces of fabric are really nice to get when you want to sew clothes for the doll. Other examples are a simple recorder or a harmonica to pick out some notes on.

War toys

At the playground a little guy ran around shooting with a big toy revolver that banged so loudly that all the children stopped their games and looked at him. A few younger children were frightened.

The boy's mother didn't know what to do. The boy had nagged her for so long—he had even awakened in the middle of the night several times and called that he wanted a gun! Now he was shooting it at other children. It didn't look very nice.

Well, what do you do in that situation?

Can a ban on the sale of war toys change people's attitudes towards them?

I think that a more important aspect of the issue is this: whole airplanes have been hijacked with toy pistols, and banks have been robbed with toy guns. Then they aren't so innocent any more. It can actually be very dangerous to wave a toy gun around in our high-strung times.

I feel it's important to teach your children to never aim anything with the character of a gun at another person. They could aim at a target board or hunt animals for food, but they should never threaten one another.

I think it's wrong to say that all children play war games, that it's natural for them. Only children raised in war-ravaged areas of the world need to play war to work through their terrible experiences.

Children who grow up in peaceful surroundings don't really have a need to war against each other, do they? But they do need excitement—to sneak up on each other, to crawl around in the dark of the night among bushes and caves, or to be in a creepy, squeaky attic.

Children who are fed with television violence do, however, need to work through those impressions. Even if they only watch peaceful programs—sweet children's movies—the passive staring of the television situation itself finally leads to dammed-up energy, which then is often released in un-controlled or aggressive behavior.

The rhythm of the year

Children want to feel longing and expectation. Annual hol-idays offer fine opportunities for making the home a little extra-exciting and festive. Even if you, as a parent, don't find any meaning in the Christmas and Easter celebrations, you can perhaps find other annually-occurring opportunities for festivity—birthdays, for example.

The birthday child is somehow honored. He can have a special birthday chair to sit on (an easy chair can be labeled the celebration-chair and dragged out into the kitchen) or get a beautiful wreath around his head. (If it's wintertime, you can make a wreath out of tissue paper or felt.) He gets waited on by everyone else and gets to request his favorite meal for dinner. He's awakened by singing and tones from the harmonica or by a birthday canon. Children then come to think that others' birthdays are wonderful, too.

Every fall and spring you can take excursions to a certain place and invite some friends, grill hot dogs and apples over a campfire, and sleep in sleeping bags.

Perhaps the most fun time for the children is the period before Christmas with its making of presents and decorations, baking, rustling, and bustling. The home is seen with new eyes as it receives a beautiful attire.

Children experience that a long year has gone by. Last year I couldn't move the rolled-out gingerbread cookies from the counter to the cookie sheet, but this year I can. Last year I couldn't reach up to the craft table, but this year I can. The joy of preparing surprises and of hoping for some for yourself is great.

A school-age child can keep busy for hours making Christmas or birthday presents! Special things can be made out of beeswax. For example, beeswax can be attached in patterns and figures to white candles. It's done fairly quickly so that the children don't tire of it, and it turns out so beautifully! Pictures to have in the window can be made by glueing tissue paper onto waxed paper; nice frames can be made for them from solid white paper.

The changes of the seasons can be the basis for almost all preschool and kindergarten activities. Songs suitable for fall, winter, spring, and summer can be sung. Grinding of grain and baking can take place during harvest time. Candles can be steeped before Christmas, little birdhouses can be made in the spring, etc. This method will help to overcome the lack of being anchored in nature's annual cycles that so many city children are likely to suffer.

Summary

During school age the child wants to get inner pictures to work with and likes to be reached via feeling and imagination.

Now come the games with rules that require the children to practice cooperating with one another.

It is not until these school years that the child is mature enough to see caricatures, since only now does it know what the caricatured person actually looks like.

We can make a soft, noncommercial alternative to Barbie & Co.

An important task for everyone who guides children is to give them responsibility for simple tasks so that they will feel themselves to be a part of the family's life and not feel banished to a corner of the nursery.

Give Johnny real tools and saucepans when he wants to do carpentry work or to cook—and real instruments when he wants to play music.

War toys are actually dangerous. Banks can be robbed with them.

We can gather many exciting ideas for activities for the children (and ourselves) from the changes of the seasons.

Toys (school age)

Suggestions:

- The small soft doll, size A, with clothes.
- Sewing things and fabric.
- Expanded collection of dress-up clothes, veils, hats, belts.
- Makeup: wax crayons, if the face is first rubbed with grease.
- Doll-house dolls, knot- or yarn dolls.
- More detailed doll-house items.
- Children can make almost anything out of beeswax.

- Wax crayons, watercolor paints, smaller paintbrushes, colored pencils.
- Pieces of wood, wooden wheels, several real tools with a safe storage place, instruction in how to care for and sharpen them.
- Pieces of fur, leather, textile glue.
- String.
- Blue clay, plaster.
- Soft and hard animals.
- Weaving loom, knitting needles, crochet hook, yarns.
- Empty boxes—can make a little theater with cardboard figure, for instance.
- Simple games: for example, Parcheesi, dominoes,
- Chinese checkers, mouse trap.

Outdoors: kites, tree houses, homemade pedal-car, high swing, own garden plot, boat, airplane, etc.

School children can make their own puzzles: paint a picture on plywood, then, using water colors, sketch out the pieces; varnish; saw out pieces with a fretsaw.

Wait until the children can manage to sit still for long periods and pick over the small parts before you give them detailed model-construction sets.

Watch out for toxic glue!

A real erector set is a wonderful (and expensive) present for a nine/ten-year-old.

At this age (9–10), he can steep pewter or plaster or form things in clay and have them fired.

It's all set—start playing!

The initiative for work and activities in the adult world often comes from the outside. Other people need the objects we make and the services we offer. We work for others.

Play is the child's work. But it can only be compared to work in that it is the child's most important and serious activity. Play is not for someone else. The child plays out of inner necessity.

When well-meaning adults come and present the child with ready-made toys, it's like coming, in a sense, with an order from the outside.

"Here you are, play with this now, just like the toy is meant to be played with!"

AV materials and preschool children

We worry that Sophie won't learn to button buttons. She has to practice! We hurry out and buy a frame with two pieces of fabric that can be buttoned together.

The purpose of the frame is to button buttons—the ability to button buttons in general, in other words! For there's no real reason for buttoning just these buttons. And Sophie discovers that after the third attempt.

To button a button usually has a purpose beyond the buttoning itself—for example, that sweater should be closed so that we aren't cold, or to keep the bonnet on. That's why it's much more fun for Sophie to naughtily button up all of mommy's coat buttons when she isn't looking—so that she has a lot of trouble getting her coat on!—or to be good and helpfully button little brother's jacket.

We're worried that little Sophie won't feel the difference between flour, sugar, and salt. We give her three identical jars containing these substances:

"Here, little Sophie, let's taste. So different, aren't they? This is salt, this is sugar, and this is flour.

Contentedly, we leave little Sophie for a moment to answer the phone. When we come back, Sophie has mixed the contents of the jars with water and is kneading this wonderful sticky mess.

"Oh!" we say. "But Sophie, now we don't know which is which any more!"

We don't see that Sophie has actually made a pie dough.

Let her learn by living; don't keep her from living by trying to teach her!

The living activities of the home, the tasks that have meaning for the adults, are the most fun for preschool children. To get your own piece of dough and make rolls is much more wonderful than to get a piece of blue-colored, salty play-dough which you can't bake or eat. Isn't it pretty strange to make a dough with real flour and salt that then can't be eaten? Why are we baking, then?

In a world where many people don't have bread for the day, it seems very bad to me to get the children used to throwing away food.

Building hiding places

The purpose of a hiding place is that you can go there and hide. It's not much fun to hide in a place in which everyone knows where you are. Then you can't pretend that you're lost, parentless, and miserable! It's not so easy to imagine that everyone cries when they discover that you're gone, if everyone knows where you are.

When Sophie has hidden herself in her secret place in the cleaning closet or in the attic, she sits there and imagines how it would be to get along all on your own, to run away and

lie hidden in the cargo space of a boat. She is in the great
security of her home and still she imagines that she has disappeared without a trace. She tries to understand her own
role within the family, who she is, and how the others view
her. She can only do that if she's in a place that no one can
suspect is a hiding place.

Replicas

Go into a toy store. Look through the whole range of mer-
chandise. How many of all these toys can actually be used
for free, creative play?

Fortunately, children are not as unintelligent as we think.
They can even rise above the fact that the toy car looks like
an exact miniature of a real car model.

Little Sophie can, with her imagination, transform the
Volvo into a Saab or into a meatball!

Don't the toy producers misdirect their diligence when
they make the toy cars into exact replicas of the real cars?
If they aren't perfect, the car producers protest and force
the toy producer to withdraw and change the model!

I think that a lot of what is served up in toy stores looks
like some kind of consolation prize for the children as com-
pensation to the poor guys for being only children! They are

given cute little miniatures of adults' belongings with which to enjoy themselves while they are waiting to get big.

But children play to develop, to exercise their senses, to grow and mature into versatile individuals.

Sophie has been given a "real" little child-sized vacuum cleaner made of plastic. It can vacuum and has cute little paper bags that go with it. Does the toy manufacturer think that Sophie will strain her imagination if she has to pretend that her vacuum cleaner vacuums up dust?

Let's see now, is it because Sophie thinks that the room is dusty that she plays at vacuuming, or is it because she wants to do like the adults, because she wants to imitate their movements?

Sometimes Sophie really does want to clean up. Then she can very well use the home's real vacuum cleaner and find joy in the result.

But another time Sophie pretends that she is mommy cleaning. First she vacuums, and then she moves around, bends down, and peeks under the bed like she's seen her mother do. She lifts things up and putters. Then she does the dishes and washes, and everything goes at full speed. Housecleaning could never go that fast. But Sophie doesn't have the ambition to make it clean. She's just playing the role of the housecleaning mother.

The artist

Imagine an artist who's working on a motif. He makes sketches and has a vision within himself that he wants to illustrate. Then a friend comes over and stands watching for a moment. Then he rushes out and returns after half an hour with a ready-made oil painting representing a similar motif to the one on which the artist is working.

"Here! Look what I bought for you. You can have it, so you won't have to work so hard on yours any more!" says the good friend generously—and expects gratefulness and happiness from the receiver.

And what does the artist do?

Of course, he smashes the donated painting over the head of the former friend. Or, if he is of a more introverted and insecure nature, he'll perhaps tear up his own sketches and stamp them into the wastebasket and avow that he should have been something other than an artist. That's exactly how I experience that the child must feel when he's given a plastic telephone just as he got immersed in playing that a string is the cord and a shoe is the receiver.

The child is an artist!

We should meet with respect his or her striving to create.

The little collector

Once I was looking in a toy store for regular white paper in large sheets—which I couldn't find, of course.

A grandmother came in to buy something for her grandchild, a boy who was turning six. The grandmother quickly checked the whole wall full of toy cars. She seemed to be well versed in the various car models. She turned with disappointment to the salesperson:

"Don't you have any more models?" she asked.

"No, but there must be something out of all this that'll be suitable?" replied the salesperson.

"Don't you have that big, new ambulance with a real siren that was supposed to come out this fall?" wondered the lady.

"No, I'm sorry, it hasn't arrived yet, but there are lots of other ambulances here... see, here's a nice plastic one with a real stretcher," the salesperson ventured.

The grandmother looked thoughtfully at the ambulance and then said:

"No, you see, my grandson already has all that and all the other models here ... he would like something new that he hasn't seen before!"

The salesperson and I looked speechlessly at the grandmother. I started to mumble something about maybe giving the boy a plain wooden car which could endlessly become all kinds of new models. But it didn't register.

This boy was obviously a victim of our modern consumer-thinking. He had been transformed from having been an artist into being a collector. His room had turned into a museum instead of being a studio.

Do children mean all they say?

Another day I went into the toy store and said I wanted a toy, but a simple thing of wood, without any details—just a bus, in other words.

The salesman frowned and then eagerly showed me all the exceptional latest bus models he had.

"And here's a Volvo, look here how real it looks. Volvo has actually approved it. Look, it's exactly like a real Volvo bus. Look out on the street yourself, and compare!"

"But I want a bus, you know, a long wooden piece with wheels under it, something that shows the characteristics of a bus—not a lot of details," I said.

The salesman looked at me as if I were distastefully starry-eyed.

"But, my dear, don't you realize we couldn't sell something like that? It has to be the real thing!" he burst out.

"You can't sell those?" I asked.

"No, no, the children want real model cars, of course. The children want to have them!" the salesman said eagerly.

I said thank-you and left.

The children want to have them. . . .

Do children actually want everything that they say they want? Do they always know what is best for them? Then parents aren't needed, are they?

A child can say that it's healthy and want to go out even though it has a fever of 102°!

"He really wants that car. Let him have it (and there won't be any clamor)," tired parents often reason. But deep inside, the child is disappointed in their lack of involvement. And then Sophie wants one car after another as soon as she is bored.

Wouldn't it be more fun to paint a little picture for Sophie, or to tie a simple knot-doll out of a handkerchief, or to help Sophie with whatever she's trying to do?

We are not cruel because we say, "No, you can't have that car," at least not if we add, "but when we get home we'll do something fun together."

The child as a consumer

There are toys for sale in a store. The toys are aimed at children. So children get toys. Sometimes children have no money. Then adults buy toys for them. Sometimes children have money. Then they themselves buy the toys.

Children want different things. So there are many different things to buy. But then the children have to choose which thing they want.

But children can't choose—they want all those things!

If we ask if they want the boat or the train, they answer—both! If we have emphasized strongly enough that they will get only one thing, they'll answer that they want one of those things. But they don't choose, they just make a guess. They chance that it's the boat they want, and they don't know if they'll regret it after they come back home. They really want both things the whole time.

As soon as Sophie comes home with the boat she starts to daydream about the train.

"Mommy ... maybe next time I can get the train?"....

Then we think she's ungrateful.

If we absolutely insist on developing our children's ability to make a choice, it's better to say, for example:

"Which sandwich are you going to eat first, the one with cheese, or the one with salami?"

The child has both sandwiches and doesn't need to relinquish either one because of her choice. When there is a choice between alternatives in which the child will only get one thing, it seems more reasonable if the adult, with his knowledge of the child, chooses on the child's behalf.

The child lives so powerfully in the present that it can't anticipate its feelings in the future—not even an hour ahead.

Perhaps it's kindest towards Sophie not to let her participate in the toy purchases until she is old enough to handle money herself and save for certain desired things.

Educational toys

There are many toys nowadays that are praised because they're so educational. What does that mean? It means that toys have an ability to guide the child so that he or she will train a certain ability.

Sophie can practice putting cubes of different sizes into corresponding holes, building a pyramid out of ever-smaller pieces, discerning a certain color or shape among many others, fitting little weights together two and two, solving all kinds of tricky tasks.

But she can also practice balancing herself by walking on a board, hitting the mark with a ball in a can, scraping out a bowl of cookie dough so that the spoon catches all the pieces of dough in the bowl.

By herself, she chooses to do these latter tasks when she feels like it, and in her own way. The prior ones are determined by ready-made material.

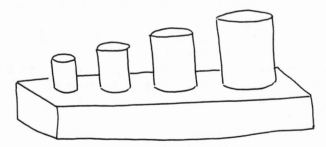

Sophie has received a board with holes of different sizes in it: a number of cylinders of corresponding thickness are to be fitted into the holes. Sophie inserts the cylinders, and the producer's mild voice can be heard from the distance.

"If you practice really diligently now, my friend, you'll see that you'll be able to put the right cylinders into the right holes within a few days."

When Sophie manages to get the cylinders down into the proper holes, the educational toy has been exhausted! And when Sophie has worked her way through the whole pedagogical material, she must be... yes, what becomes of her?

Oh, but don't be so extreme, somebody says. Nobody goes and buys the full line of educational toys. Not even a daycare center could afford that. It can't hurt for the child to have a few different ones, can it?

No, it might not hurt, but of what use are they? We arbitrarily pick out and develop certain of all the possible abilities that the child is to learn. Why can't we just as well let the children help themselves to the tasks that life offers and devote themselves to those?

Man is very adaptable. He can be trained to do almost anything, especially as a child. But doesn't that happen at the expense of other abilities?

If children are trained early in a one-sided way, don't they then lose the versatility so characteristic of man? Doesn't early training encroach on their imaginativeness and their emotional maturity?

I don't think Sophie needs a piece of wood with different sized holes and cylinders to learn to estimate the sizes of

holes and cylinders.

She can put lipstick into its casing, chapstick into another, a pencil into a bottle, an empty baking powder can into an empty cocoa can.

Sophie can try the baby-food lid on the powder jar; she can put all the saucepans inside one another according to size and put all the jar lids in a row. She can put Grandpa's hat on the sofa pillow. And besides, by putting her little hand into every little hole she's found, she's been practicing to judge distance and size ever since she was a baby.

Sophie was perhaps just getting involved with practicing a difficult balancing-act on the threshold, or with finding out whether the big pillow falls down from the upper bunk faster than the little feather, when in we come and present her with our exciting wrapped package, with which she's to sort shapes and learn math.

And, good as Sophie is, she busies herself with the "educational" task. She forgets her own tasks, for she lives in the present.

We adults often feel that puzzles—especially the end-product, the finished puzzles—are so satisfying. You can see the results.

But pillow and feather on the floor we call a Messy Room.

A continual teetering on the chair at the supper table we call Bad Tablemanners (in spite of its being a great balance training).

A constant creeping around on the floor and a tripping along on tiptoes we call Don't-You-Have-Anything-To-Do? We can't see that it's Investigation-Of-How-Long-I-Am-When-I-Lie-Down and Balance-Training-On-Tiptoes.

One can only hope that Sophie forgives us our limited perspective!

Summary

Play is the child's work. But it's work that the child performs for itself; it plays for the sake of its own development.

But when Sophie pretends to cook food she doesn't need a true-to-life miniature stove, which will only impede her imagination. A box is quite good enough.

The child can be compared to an artist. Through playing, it shapes its experience of life. With ready-made, formed toys we direct the child's creativity; we force our opinions on the child.

Many children have been transformed from being creative artists into being collectors of things.

Do children always know what's best for them?

Never expose the child to a choice-situation in which it will only get one thing. It's better that you choose for the child!

Let Sophie live, play freely, rather than directing her into intellectual problem-solving that requires her to sit still.

Sophie prescribes her own tasks that are important for her; don't divert her from that.

The child who can't play

Conrad

It's Sunday. The family is home. But little Conrad can't play. He can't motivate himself to do anything. Everything is "blah."

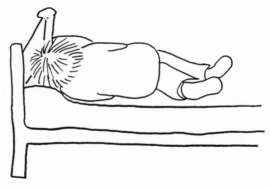

Conrad is six years old. He just lies on his bed with his face towards the wall, sucks his thumb, and occasionally makes disturbing noises.

What would you do to make him feel like playing?

Here are some possible alternatives:

1. Nag:
   "Don't just lie there and complain all day, do something!"

2. Go to Conrad, sit down next to him, stroke him, ask him:
   "What's wrong, my dear? Did something happen in

school last week? Is there something you want? Have I said something wrong? Are you in a bad mood? Are you mad at Daddy? Are you having a hard time with Little Brother? Do you have a tummyache? But tell me what's the matter, don't just yell at me! Answer! What's wrong with you? Can't I help you?"

3. Rush into Conrad's room, take out the building set, cheerfully start building, and eagerly say:
   "Come see what a fine steam shovel we'll build!"

4. Sit down in another room and start thinking: Does Conrad possibly watch too much television (which can make him passive, as has been proven)? Does he ever see adults who perform their practical tasks wholeheartedly? Is he allowed to take part in our tasks? Does he participate in our lives at all? Does he know where Daddy works, and with what? Does he know where his teacher and/or day-care personnel live, what their homes are like? Does he know his nearest neighbor? Does Conrad have material for creative play? Maybe he has too many things?

5. Start an interesting task, for example, fixing the window-hasp that has been broken for six months. Utter concerned little words about how difficult it is. Complain that a certain tool is lacking— Imagine how easy it would be if I had a pair of pliers —which Conrad has.

ONE: The first alternative is, of course, not too successful. Nagging seldom brings results.

TWO: To sit quietly with Conrad and stroke him is nice. Then he feels that we care about him and understand him. But we don't have to say anything. If we sit with him quietly, there is a chance that Conrad himself will start talking about his problems. If we shower him with questions, he'll only get confused. Everything sounds equally plausible in his ears.
   The more he thinks about his condition, the more worried

he becomes. He thinks that this must be something serious. He'll probably choose several of our initial suggestions.

"Yes, I'm mad at you and Daddy, and Little Brother is stupid and I have a tummyache and school is no fun."

But maybe none of these is the real reason for the lousy mood.

A young child shouldn't have to analyze his life situation. He wants to live with spontaneity. If Conrad becomes too conscious of himself, he becomes affected and tries a lot of tricks to get our attention.

THREE: It's good to play with the child's toys, since it's an act—something which, for children, is better than words. But then it has to come out of an honest urge to play.

If we are making an effort to play, Conrad probably senses our duplicity. If we always crawl around on the floor and honk and buzz, there's a risk that we'll be considered as a clown or as something to climb on. The children can become totally dependent on our assistance in order to be able to play. Or they can be led to excitedly jump on and cling to us, to pinch and tickle us, and to test the limits of our patience in every way. But they do this with a certain inner discomfort, for they want to be able to admire us.

FOUR and FIVE could very well be combined. They are, in my opinion the best alternatives.

Think back every day on the day which has passed and try to see little Conrad in front of you: how did he look today, how did he move, how did his voice sound? We don't have to find a scapegoat for why things went wrong. That doesn't help anyone. But just to see Conrad in front of us, without analyzing, helps us to get a much better contact with him the following day.

The same, by the way, is valid with respect to all the people with whom we associate. We can often discover something in our way of being that we can change. Maybe we ourselves are bored? If we can't get ourselves to do anything, it's not so strange if Conrad also is bored.

Or has Conrad watched so much television that he's

forgotten what it is to play? Has he gotten used to always being entertained? There are many TV-damaged children who
can't play anymore. Medicine: total prohibition of TV-watch-
ing until about twelve years of age.

Or maybe Conrad has so many toys that he literally drowns
in the hopeless mess in his room? Does he have any friends?

Maybe he turns his back towards his untidy room because
it's hard for him to face the mess. Then we can suggest:

"Should I help you clean up and sort out all the things you've
outgrown and those that are broken?"

We can put those things in a box in the attic.

If Conrad feels too lonely in his room, we can bring the
ironing board in there and do ironing, or carry in an easy
chair and sit next to him and read or sew. It's always more
fun to do things near other people. Conrad has always made
an effort to drag his toys along with him to the room where
we're working, so as to be able to be near us—perhaps we
should show him that we also want to be near him sometimes?
Or he can invite the whole family to afternoon tea in his
room and make a nice arrangement there.

A six-year-old often can't resist responding when mother
or father appear clumsy and ignorant, so that it can show
them that it knows how things are done. If the child could
assist with a pair of pliers to solve the whole problem with
a window-hasp, it probably would. And before the child
withdraws again, we suggest something else that needs fixing or arranging. Maybe we could rearrange the furniture
in Conrad's room or go up to the attic to get something?
He'll get going and feel revived.

It's not always so easy. Many children today suffer from
something we could call weakening of the will. They are so
tired and unenterprising. They can't come up with things to
do, and they require constant entertainment. They need to
exercise the will by finishing what they've started, and they
must be inspired by their environment to take their own
initiative.

Such children should never have to hear a NO! when they've
thought of something they want to do. But in our dangerous
and child-hostile world they are stopped everywhere. They

should have a woodsy slope where they can go often and play in greater freedom. They need to participate in happy song hours, to see craftsmen at work, to perform little "assignments" on their own, to have a cozy and happy home.

The will can be developed, just like thinking and feeling.

Full of imagination—or phantoms?

Then we have little Nicky. He is so imaginative, we say nervously as he comes running with his hair on end, rushing around like a whirlwind, poking into everything, shaking out of eagerness, and talking incessantly:

"And then we flew away on a moonrocket and then it crashed like THhiis and everything went CRAsh, BOOoom, but we came down anyway, and ... oh, what a great stiletto, WOW, snap like THIS, swish! That's cool—oh, boy, it got stuck in the chair! Neat, what a cool knife! And now I'd like to have the world's fastest racing car and just go flying into the finish—oh, Mom, I'm so hungry, I want a sandwich, aren't we going to eat soon? And you know what, Mom, yesterday there was a guy who kicked me right here...."

Nicky can't play, either. He's not creating anything particularly original with his thoughts. He's actually not very imaginative.

He apparently gets too many impressions. He's insecure and unsure of himself. He has to use violence to prove himself. He's very susceptible to the element of violence, some of which comes to him through television.

Impressions dance a literal witches' dance in his head. He doesn't know what to do with them. The only way he can get to know and to defend himself against these phantoms is to try to express them in words. Then he can objectify them to his thinking.

He wants Mom to hear all the terrible things he says. He wants her to know what's going on inside him. He doesn't intend to frighten; on the contrary, he wants Mom to take the phantoms away and give him warmth and love (food) instead. That's why he's constantly pouring out all the swear-words and bad words that he's carrying around. If the scary things are given names, they become more manageable.

Just like other children, Nicky wants the world to be good. If the contrary is proven to him again and again, his inner balance is disturbed and his will to live is damaged. He wants to be happy. Can't we let him be happy while he's little?

If he's spared when he's young from getting so many ter-rible experiences through facts and pictures in newspapers and on television, his will to change the conditions of the world will strengthen as he grows older. Then he has energy left over to feel sympathy and to develop understanding.

But if the world is soon going to explode in a nuclear war, it's no fun to play any more.

If we want Nicky to be in harmony with himself and to have a rich imagination, we can't talk to him as we would to an adult. We can't put part of the responsibility on him. We have to keep the burdensome and the serious to ourselves as long as he's little.

I don't mean that we have to hold our hands in front of the child's eyes as soon as reality appears negative. The child has the right to know more about sad events that happen to us personally. They are realities which affect us, and we have to live with them.

The fairytale—our inner reality

Fairytales contain many fine examples of how the evil within us is fought against and how our good sides win. If only we ourselves take the tales seriously, children get much joy from hearing again and again how the good within us wins. They can then listen without fear to the most horrifying stories about wolves eating children and trolls who petrify princes.

The children intuitively sense that the story isn't about real wolves (nothing bad to be said about them!), but about our own voracious instincts, that within us which has the character of beasts of prey.

But if the person who reads the story doesn't see any deeper symbolism in it and takes the troll for only a figment of the imagination and the castle for royalistic propaganda, well, then the value of the tale for the child is not as great. The child will then have nightmares about the fairytales, just as it does about other dangerous and inexplicable things.

When the person telling the story feels open to the possibility of there being an ancient wisdom and knowledge about man's soul concealed in the folktale, it can then have a strongly positive influence—for all tales have a happy ending. They want to show that in all difficult inner struggles, the good in humanity will conquer.

I have many times heard the opinion that it's not right to tell romantic stories to children of today, because children don't live like that any longer. Disregarding the fact that there are children of today who do live in idyllic environments, I think that most children live in a little house in their inner landscape. You can see it in their drawings.

The house often symbolizes the child's own body. Even children raised in apartments live in cabins within themselves. Not until they get older do they move out into the wide reality, and only then will they also draw all kinds of houses.

Fairytales take place in the human interior. We all have a wicked stepmother within us who selfishly looks at the mirror; we all have trolls and dragons and dark forces which lurk in the depths and try to overpower the prince, our ego.

Sometimes we calculate coldly—and then the ice-being comes with his entourage to envelop the landscape of our soul with snow.

If we feel warmth of heart and sacrifice ourselves for others, we gain entry to the orchard laden with fruit, and the prince and the princess are united. Two sides of our personality are united in harmony.

It's actually wrong to let children watch wars and violence on television for the supposed reason that that's how it is in our world. For the majority of the children who sit and watch TV it is not so. There is no war on the street outside our house.

It's this small, limited world that belongs to the child. For the child, the other side of the world is something very foreign, distant, and incomprehensible. But the other side of the street is something totally comprehensible.

Television practically never shows anything that has to do with the child's reality. The TV programs touch neither upon the child's outside home environment nor upon the inner personal relationships with which only those close to him or her are familiar.

To give children realistic everyday stories in books with the motivation that that's how many children today live—that Charlie lives in an apartment building, that his mother and father often fight, that this is what it's like to be in a hospital or at the dentist's or in a barn or in Antarctica—is actually to fool both ourselves and the child. No film or book can show a child how it is. Only the reality that we ourselves experience can show us the workings of the outside world.

And if we want to show children the workings of the human inner reality, we do so best by telling fairytales and little stories of our own, and by listening to the child's questions. The child can carry along and grow with those images painted in words in the fairytales. They can help the child to struggle along with his own difficulties.

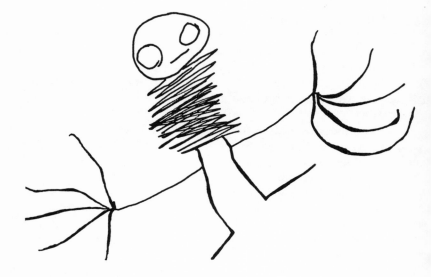

A three-year-old's version of the child stretching out his tentacles.

The child can dare to stretch out his feelers in the positive atmosphere of the fairytales. But if he meets pessimism and misery again and again, he will pull in his tentacles, close himself up, and suck his thumb; he won't want to grow up, or he may devote himself to idol worship.

Nicky can't play. What can we do to help him? If his faith in people has been disturbed it can take us many years to build up an atmosphere of joyful and earnest living around him. We must meet all his calls for help, all his babble, with calm attentiveness and try to reach what is behind him:

"Stiletto, did you say, what's that? Have you ever seen one of those?" we ask.

Perhaps it comes out that Nicky has been frightened by an older boy with a stiletto. If we talk about it, Nicky feels calmer. He hears us say the dangerous words and the phantoms are brought down to earth, played down.

But we should never try to force Nicky to say something; then he'll feel interesting just because of his flow of bad words.

We can try to interest him in doing practical things with his hands: scrub, wash windows, bake, knead clay, saw and nail, paint furniture and pictures!

It's nice to show him our understanding of his fears in a roundabout way. We can tell stories about boys who go out into the fearful world and dare to meet dragons and other terrifying things, and how they finally get the princess.

Nicky doesn't get overpowered by the images from the fairytales that appear inside him, but he does get overpowered by television's moving, "real" images.

He can protect himself against the images from the tale. He makes the dragon only as scary as he can handle in his inner vision.

But on TV the dragon looks scary, and our eyes tell us that it's really alive. If it's so terrible that Nicky gets scared, there's nothing we can do; he has already seen it, and the picture in the mind can't be erased.

Television's images force themselves upon him and populate his brain to such an extent that he can't defend himself.

For his impressions to become an inner reality for him, he needs to be protected from a noisy environment and allowed time to digest them at his own pace.

Summary

Conrad can't play. He withdraws, is passive.

If we quietly analyze his whole situation instead of shower-ing questions on him, Conrad will at least sense our involve-ment, and he won't have to analyze his condition himself.

Speak to Conrad with actions instead of with words if he is under seven. The very best way for parents to awaken his interest is to make themselves very busy with something and to constantly mutter about how complicated and difficult it is.

His will to follow through on games and ideas can be developed.

Nicky has received too many impressions. He can't bring any order into them. He's overpowered by "phantoms" (iso-lated fragments of his memory) from TV programs, his own experiences, comics, etc., that whirl around without any relation in his memory.

"Clean up" his experiences. Decrease TV watching to none at all! Give him inner images to busy himself with instead of outer ones—fairytales, your own made-up stories, living time together with other children and adults, as calm a daily program as possible.

Try to anchor Nicky's life to the here and now. Let him experience for himself rather than receive filmed second-hand experiences. Let him help with practical things at home as much as possible. Sit him down to do something with his hands—knead clay, saw, bake, paint!

2

About wool

Wool's ability to warm is well known. Because of the waviness of the long, thin fibers, lots of tiny air-pockets are created inside the wool.

Wool retains the warmed air, but allows it to circulate so that it isn't confined. Wool can also absorb moisture up to one-third of its weight. So the wool doll feels warm and alive in the child's arms.

Wool fibers are more elastic than any synthetic fiber. If bent, they strive to get back to their original position. The doll keeps its shape. Only if it's been washed in water that is too hot does wool lose its elasticity and get matted together, possibly creating lumps.

Wool fleece is an environmentally-sound, natural material which is less flammable and has less static electricity than synthetic materials do.

It's cheapest to buy fleece directly from a sheep owner. Just make sure that you don't get the very dirtiest abdominal fleece!

Then wash the fleece gently in lukewarm water with soap or ammonia. This is a fun job for little children! Rinse it several times and then spread it out in the sun, or on a towel on the drying rack.

If you have fine fleece of good quality, simply fluff it up by separating the wool tufts with your hands. Otherwise, the fleece should be carded. Carding brushes can be purchased in weaving shops or loom factories.

Children from about the age of five can help to card, but it takes time. To card enough fleece to stuff a medium-sized doll could take two hours!

Work with small tufts of fleece. Move the carding brushes

parallel to each other.

You can buy washed and carded fleece (sometimes as seconds) from spinning mills, yarn or loom stores, and sometimes also in other stores.

If you can't manage to buy any fleece, you can hunt up all kinds of wool scraps. Try cutting wool sweaters and socks into pieces and rolling them up so that they can be stuffed into the doll's body, legs, or arms. Take an old ball of woolen yarn for the head. Woolen yarn bought on sale might be about the same price as store-bought carded fleece.

Use colorfast yarn!

Children who are allergic to wool can get a doll stuffed with cotton waste or polyester batting, or with synthetic yarns and sweaters.

For washing instructions, please see page 172.

Knot-dolls

The knot-doll is suitable as an infant's first doll and is a simple doll for all ages.

Doll with head of knotted fabric

<u>Materials</u>:

- Square piece of a <u>very</u> thin and flexible plain cotton or silk fabric, or a veil.
- Tuft of fleece for hair or beard.
- Triangular piece of fabric for a kerchief or an apron.

Fig. 1a

Fig. 1b

<u>To make the doll</u>:

Take a pinch of the material at "x", as in figure 1, and lift up. Then tie the point that is created into a simple knot. This knot will be the head.

Now find the two shortest corners that hang below the head. Tie knots in them also. Now the doll has hands.

Fig. 2

The two remaining corners are knotted into feet, unless the doll is to have a long skirt. See figure 2.

If you stuff a little fleece in under the head-knot, the doll will be an old man. Add a piece of fabric as a kerchief or an apron and the doll is an old woman!

In a brief flourish, the doll has been created as the child (ren) watched. Older children can now make more of them.

Doll with ball head

<u>Materials:</u>

- Square piece of plain cotton fabric, possibly skin-colored tricot (cotton knit). A handkerchief would also do.
- Washed fleece to stuff the head with. (Cotton batting would be all right, but then the doll can't be washed.)
- Cotton rug warp or cotton twine to tie with.
- Colored pencil or needle and thread to mark eyes, mouth, and hair.
- Pieces of fabric for clothes, if desired.

<u>To make the doll:</u>

Put a ball of fleece (or batting) on top of the square fabric

at "x" as in figure 1a. Gather the fabric around the ball, wrap
the string tightly around the neck, and tie a knot in the string.
The ball is the head.

We already have a very simple doll, suitable for an infant.
If we want to make the doll more distinctive, we can indicate
hands and feet with knots, as below in figure 3.

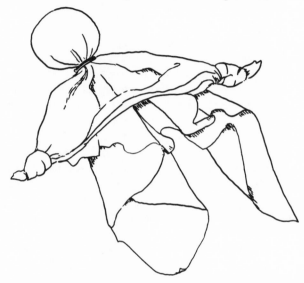

Fig. 3

Wrap a thread around the waist and crosswise over the
chest (see photo on p. 18). This doll can be varied:

Drape a little fleece over the head, attach it with some
stitches that form a part in the middle—and the doll is a
little girl!

Wrap a piece of fabric a few turns around the doll's body,
right under the arms. Tie a thread or a band around that,
sew a few strands of hair onto the head—and you have a baby!

Fig. 4

This little doll-baby can be made so tiny that it can sleep

on a bed of fleece in a walnut shell.

Knot-doll marionette

Materials:

- Same as for the previous doll, plus two little pebbles to use as weights in the hands.
- Long threads with which to suspend it.
- A little veil, a golden band, a pearl, or any other adornment which would indicate the doll's character.

To make the doll:

Make a knot-doll with a ball head. If you use very elastic fabric, the doll will move very nicely. Sew little pebbles into the hands.

Sew on hair of fleece or thread. Sew on little dots as eyes and a mouth.

Hang a veil over the doll's shoulders, or adorn it in other ways.

Fig. 5

Attach threads to the hands. Attach one also to each side of the head—otherwise the doll will easily twist around. Let the threads be quite short, so that a child can move the doll. If the threads from the hands are put together—and the threads from the head, too—no cross is needed. The doll is held by the threads.

These simple puppets can be used throughout the preschool and kindergarten years. School-age children can make them themselves and set up little routines with them.

Doll-house doll

A NOTE ON MEASUREMENTS:

Measurements of the dolls and materials in this book were originally laid out in the metric system. The "conversions" of centimeters to inches, grams to ounces, etc. , that appear throughout the remainder of the book are not intended to be exact. Instead, they have been slightly modified in order to provide the non-metric dollmaker with more convenient measurements than exact equivalents would allow.

Materials:

- Small square (for example 15 cm. x 15 cm. —approx. 6 x 6 in.) of skin-colored fabric, as thin as possible.
- Washed wad of fleece for head, hands, and feet.
- Strong thread to tie with.
- Fabric for coveralls or sack, for example, cotton flannel or felt.
- Needle and thread for hair, eyes, and mouth.

To make the doll:

Make a tiny (at the most 10 cm.—4 in.—tall) knot-doll with a ball head.

Make a tiny ball furthest-out in every corner for hands and feet.

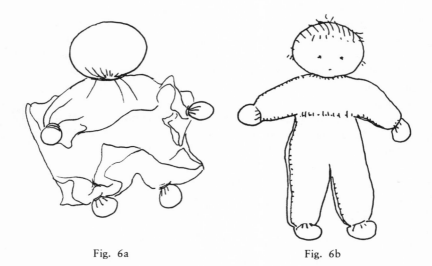

Fig. 6a   Fig. 6b

Sew a coverall right onto the doll: put two square pieces as front and back, fold in the seam allowances, and sew the shoulder seams; sew around the neck, cut in for the arms, and cut a wedge between the legs; sew up the sides and between the legs.

Mark the eyes and mouth if you wish.

Sew on some strands of hair. See figure 6b.

If you're making a baby in a sleeping sack, sew together two square pieces into a sack with the same width as the distance between the doll's outstretched hands. Turn the sack and put the doll into it so that the hands are furthest-up in the corners. Fold in the seam allowance and sew together on top of the arms and around the neck.

Stitch in a thread on the bottom, gather together, and tie a bow.

You can also stitch a thread around the chest and gather the fabric a little, so that the baby lifts its arms slightly upwards. See figure 8.

All these knot-dolls can be varied endlessly!

A doll-house doll can be made as any of a number of little characters: baker, hunter, king, nurse, grandmother, etc.

But don't give in to the temptation of making them into miniatures with detailed facial features, glasses, mustaches,

112

Fig. 7

A tiny doll for the doll house, 7 cm. (2¾ in.) tall, made like a knot-doll from a piece of fabric, four little tied balls, and sewn-on pajamas. By using other clothes, we can get different professions or characters from fairytales.

113

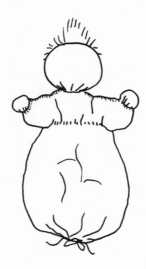

Fig. 8

shoelaces, waistcoat pockets, and the like—not if little children are to play with them, anyway.

It's enough to sew on ONE pearl! Then you've indicated that it's a princess. A white hat makes a baker. Put on a little tail—and it's a troll!

Since the nice thing with these simple knot-dolls is that they are so stimulating to the imagination, let's not make them too detailed.

It's another matter if school-age children themselves embroider on little details—then they are being creative!

You can also make a knot-doll by sewing together two potholders and attaching them to a ball. Wind and tie yarn around the four corners and then gather the waist.

See figure 9!

Fig. 9

Fig. 10

This sack doll (30 cm.—about 12 in.—tall) can be made in one evening. It's soft and nice for a 2—3 year old to sleep with. If the child so desires, the sack can be cut up to make legs.

Sack doll

This doll is appropriate as a first doll for the little child.

Materials:

- Soft, durable fabric in a bright, cheerful color. For example, 40 x 40 cm. (about 16 x 16 in.).
- Skin-colored cotton knit, about 32 x 15 cm. (12 1/2 x 6 in.)—or a light brown cotton sock.
- Woolen yarn for hair, about 25 grams (less than 1 oz.).
- Washed fleece (or woolen yarn or leftover woolen fabric) to stuff the doll with, about 200 grams (7 oz.).
- Cotton rug warp.
- Needle and thread in the color of the fabric, and in other colors for eyes and mouth.
- Sewing machine.

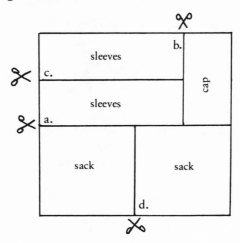

Fig. 11

To make the doll:

Cut the square of fabric in the middle "a." Fold at "b," and cut a small piece for the cap. Then fold at "c" and cut two long and narrow pieces for the sleeves. See figure 11.

Finally, cut across the remaining large piece "d" so that you get two square pieces for the sack.

Sew the top edges of the sleeves by putting the right sides of the pieces together and stitching on the machine, but leave the middle third open as the neck opening.

Sew a gathering stitch on one side of each sack piece, and gather to about one-third of the length of the sleeve piece.

Put together the right sides of the sack piece and one of the folded-out sleeve pieces and attach by machine. Attach the other half. See figure 12a.

Fold the whole piece so that the right sides come together. See figure 12b.

Fig. 12a   Fig. 12b

Attach by stitching one machine-seam that starts at one sleeve, turns down to the sack, rounds the corners, and then goes up again along the second sleeve. Leave the sleeve ends open for the hands.

Turn the sack and sleeves and stuff fleece into the bottom of the sack.

118

The head:

Cut two squares of at least 5 x 5 cm. (2 x 2 in.) from the cotton knit to use for hands.

Make a long, narrow pouch (long enough to make a head and go down into the bottom of the sack) with the remaining cotton knit by stitching it on the machine. (Or cut off the foot of the sock and tie up one end.)

Turn the pouch and tightly stuff the head part of it with fleece (or leftover woolens or old wool yarn). Hold it behind the sack body to see if it makes a head of the right size. If it seems too small or too narrow, you could either sew a wider pouch, or sew a smaller sack body.

Stuff the rest of the pouch full of fleece and tie up at the bottom. Tie off at the neck with strong rug warp.

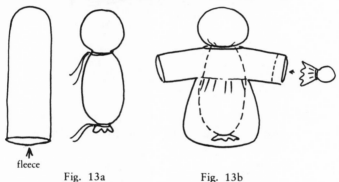

fleece

Fig. 13a   Fig. 13b

The rest of the long tricot pouch becomes the inner body. It's good if it goes all the way down, so that the doll doesn't end up having an empty stomach after a while!

Choose the least-wrinkled side of the head for a face and stuff the inner body into the sack. Fill out the sack with more fleece around the inner body. Remember that wool compresses.

Attach the outside fabric to the neck by hand. Use doubled thread or extra-strong thread—keep in mind the wear and tear to come!

Make two little ball-hands out of the skin fabric you cut earlier (or the sock foot if you used a sock). Make them at the same time so that they will be equal in size. Stuff fleece into the sleeves.

Fold in the seam allowance at the end of the sleeves, making sure that the doll's arms don't get too long. By hand, stitch a gathering seam right on the fold, and put in the hands. See figure 13b. Pull the gathering thread and sew on well.

Check the doll's proportions, compare with figure 14.

Fig. 14

You may mark the eyes and mouth with a few stitches. Place the eyes about midway in the face: children have high foreheads.

Insert the needle from the back of the head and then sew two or three stitches. Stitch across to the second eye, sew an equal number of stitches, and come out with the needle at the back of the head again.

You sew the mouth after doing the eyes, as it's then easier to find the midpoint between them. The three dots should form an equilateral triangle.

Attach hair to make tousled bangs. Lay a layer of wool yarn above the forehead and attach it with a transverse seam. If you use a wool thread, the hair will stay on better.

Sew a cap out of the remaining piece of the sack fabric. If there isn't enough, you can make a soft little cap out of a cut-off leg.

The sack doll is now finished!

120

Coverall doll

A doll suited for younger children!

Fig. 15

Model with gathered waist

<u>Materials</u>: see sack doll, page 117.

<u>To make the doll</u>:

This model is made in much the same way as the sack doll

in the previous example. The difference is only that here
you cut the sack in two, so that there will be legs.

Fig. 16

When you sew together the front and back pieces, leave the
leg-bottoms open and sew a seam on the inside of the legs.

Turn and stuff the legs well with fleece. The inner pouch
must be made shorter than the one used for the sack doll. Put
it into the body, stuff fleece around it, sew on the head, etc.

The feet can be made like the hands—like little balls. Or,
if the fabric in the legs is long enough, sew it together as in
the next example.

Model with smooth waist

Materials:

- Wool yarn to knit with, or elastic wool fabric (for ex-
  ample, an old discarded sweater) to sew with.
- Skin-colored cotton knit, about 25 x 15 cm. (6 x 10 in.).
- Or use a light brown sock.
- Washed, carded fleece, about 200 grams (approx. 7 oz.).
- Rug warp or sailmaker's twine.
- Needle and thread—one color for eyes, one for mouth,
  and a third for sewing the seams on the fabric.

122

- Yarn of contrasting color for hair.

Fig. 17

To make the doll:

Project the pattern below onto a large piece of paper. In this suggested size the upper edge is 30 cm. (12 in.). This distance is also the length from the neckhole down to the foot. The legs are half as long—15 cm. (6 in.). The legs should be a little wider than the arms, about 12 cm. (4 3/4 in.).

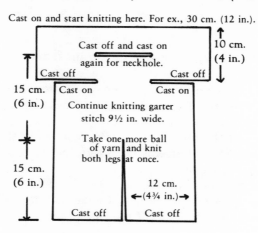

Fig. 18

Cast on stitches and knit a sample in garter stitch; measure against the pattern so that you get 30 cm. (12 in.).

Use a soft yarn of medium weight. The whole coverall is knitted in one piece. When you get to the neckhole, cast off about the middle third of the stitches; in the next row, cast on the same amount. At the slits in the sides, cast off one-third in each side and then cast on enough stitches in the next row to make the piece 24 cm. (9 1/2 in.) wide. Knit the legs at the same time with a ball of yarn for each so that they end up the same length.

Or cut out a piece of fabric which is 30 x 35 cm. (12 x 14 in.). Measure against the pattern!

You now have the cut-out or knitted piece ready. Decide which is the right side. Fold the upper edge down, as pictured, so that the neckhole is furthest-up. Stitch the sleeves with the right sides together.

Fig. 19a   Fig. 19b

Fold the legs together. Stitch the inseams of the legs—see figure 19b—and sew up to the sleeve piece.

There is one more hole. We can turn the body through it and use it to stuff fleece through if the neckhole is too small.

The head: as for the sack doll.

In this doll the inner pouch only reaches to the crotch. You can also make a bound-off head like the one described for the dress-up doll on page 136.

The hands: ball hands or a little "mitten" made of the same fabric as the head, filled with fleece and then stitched on.

The feet: ball feet, or if the fabric in the legs is long, you can just sew it up. Pinch together the bottom of each leg so that the side seams meet. Stitch together as in figure 20.

Front view   Side view (inseam)

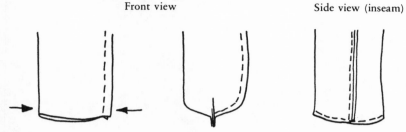

Fig. 20

Check the proportions of the doll. With outstretched arms, the doll should be able to "stand" in an egg:

Fig. 21

The hair: see the sack doll! Sew hair all over the head even if you want a cap or hat. If the cap were to be torn off, it wouldn't look so nice for the doll to be semi-bald!

The eyes: just indicate them with little dots near the middle of the face.

The mouth: make it the third corner of an equilateral triangle (with the eyes).

Please don't embroider nostrils, eyebrows, and wrinkles! Give the child's imagination room to play; just suggest the doll's face.

Also, it's better not to sew a multitude of decorations—laces, ribbons, belts, and frills—on these simple dolls.

The coverall doll is finished!

Fig. 22

A little green yarn doll, the hunter's wife in a country landscape or the little girl in a doll house, about 10 cm. (4 in.) tall. It's made with a not-too-thick wool yarn. You can also make little gnomes or Santa's helpers for the Christmas tree with this method.

Yarn doll

A doll suitable for a little landscape and for a doll house, as shown in figure 22, or for a Christmas manger and Christmas tree ornaments.

Materials:

- 25 grams (just under an ounce) of a thin, firm wool yarn (often enough for two dolls).
- Darning needle.
- Piece of cardboard, for example, 9 x 11 cm. (about 3 1/2 x 4 1/4 in.).
- Some felt, a needle, and thread for the clothes.
- Some contrasting wool yarn for hair.

To make the yarn doll:

Wind the yarn around the length of the piece of cardboard, as in figure 23a. Wind two separate sections with an equal

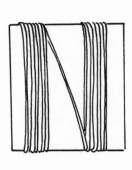

Fig. 23a

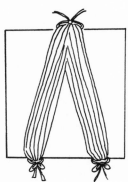

Fig. 23b

number of threads in each, for example, forty threads each. This will become head, body, and legs. Tie a little bow around the threads at the bottom of each section (feet). Push the two sections together into one at the top, and tie them together with a knot. Push the yarn off the cardboard.

The head: Wind up a small head out of yarn or washed fleece. Put it in under the "head knot" and spread the yarn around the little ball; make sure that the ball doesn't show. See figure 24a.

Thread the darning needle with a long piece of yarn. Start by winding the end of the yarn several turns around the doll's neck (right under the head). Attach by stitching through the neck a few times. Leave the yarn end hanging.

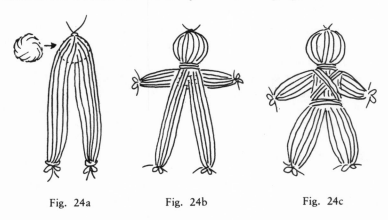

Fig. 24a   Fig. 24b   Fig. 24c

The arms: Wind the same number of threads of yarn around the width of the cardboard piece as you gave each section of the body, for example, forty. Tie up with a bow at each end and push the yarn off the cardboard.

Put the arms into the body just under the head. Take the loose yarn-end from the neck and wind it crosswise over the chest—see figures 24b and 24c—and waist of the doll. Attach by stitching a few stitches. Cut off the leftover yarn-end.

Hands and feet: Remove the bows, put a crochet hook, a knitting needle, or something similar into the loop at the end, and wind the yarn a few turns next to the loop.

Fig. 25

Now the yarn doll is finished!

You can make a variation by sewing on some hair and giving it felt clothes—add a simple cape and you have a shepherd for the Christmas manger! It's easy to put a staff into the doll's hand.

For Christmas we make red yarn dolls, and add a red felt cap for little elves. If you cut up the legs, you get a skirt for the little girl elf.

Older children can sew felt clothes by themselves.

Fig. 26

Dress-up doll

This is a doll made with skin-colored cotton knit. It can be made in a variety of sizes. By reducing the pattern here in the book, you can make it a doll-house doll. The smallest pattern given here can be an alternative to Barbie. The medium-sized dolls can become beloved bedmates for many years. The largest doll can be a baby doll, or a sturdy doll for a preschooler.

Fig. 27

Please note that the pattern in this book is a suggested one! There are many other ways of sewing cloth dolls.

Throughout the ages, long before the arrival of the plastic doll, dolls were made at home. All kinds of materials were used; one took what was available in the home, and each doll was unique.

A soft cloth doll can be made according to the descriptions that follow. But it is my hope that if you enjoy sewing dolls you will soon design your own pattern!

Materials:

- Skin-colored cotton, or even better, wool knit (for instance, cotton interlock).
- Washed and carded fleece to stuff the doll. Children who are allergic to wool can get a doll stuffed with cotton waste, viscose rayon, ramie roving, or synthetic fibers.
- Yarn for hair. Thin woolen yarns are suitable, for example, thin weaving yarn or mohair. (Use cotton yarn for children who are allergic to wool.)
- Tube gauze, size no. 2 (or regular white cotton knit) for arm, foot, and inner head. (Tube gauze is a tubular cotton gauze. You can find it at medical supply stores, and sometimes at pharmacies.)
- Cotton rug warp or sailmaker's twine for binding off the head, etc.
- Skin-colored sewing thread, embroidery thread, or yarn for eyes and mouth.
- Darning needle, strong sewing needle, sewing machine with European-size needle no. 70 or U.S. sizes 10—12.

It's nice to choose colors for the skin, hair, and eyes that match the child's. For dark brown cotton knit, look for old brown T-shirts or undershorts! Or dye some cotton knit fabric yourself.

If you like to recycle, you can use an old pink undershirt or old woolen underwear. Old stockings can also be used.

Amount of material needed:

Measurements for four different doll sizes follow. The amount of material needed depends upon which size you make.

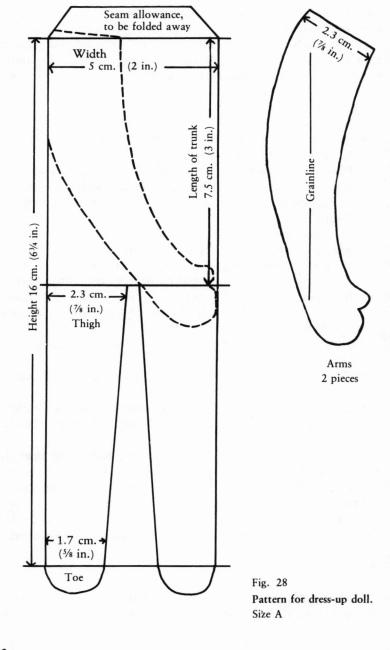

Seam allowance, to be folded away

Width
5 cm. (2 in.)

Length of trunk 7.5 cm. (3 in.)

Height 16 cm. (6¾ in.)

2.3 cm. (⅞ in.)
Thigh

1.7 cm. (⅝ in.)

Toe

2.3 cm. (⅞ in.)

Grainline

Arms
2 pieces

Fig. 28
Pattern for dress-up doll.
Size A

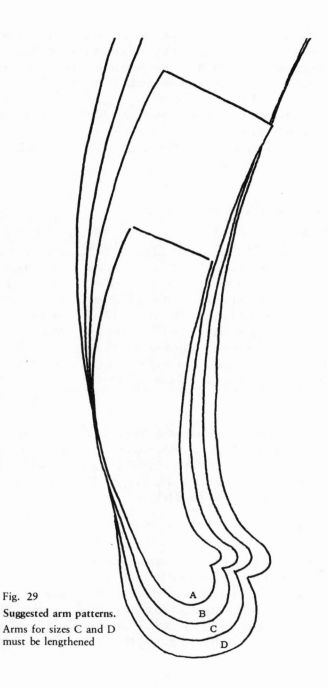

Fig. 29

Suggested arm patterns.

Arms for sizes C and D must be lengthened

A
B
C
D

Depending upon the doll maker, the same pattern can result in totally different dolls. The fleece can be stuffed tightly or loosely into the doll, the fabric can be more or less elastic, and the hair can be made in many different ways.

Save any leftover fabric—you can probably make one more very small doll out of it!

Please note the direction of the grain of the fabric when you place the pattern on it.

Table 1: Approximate amounts of materials

Doll Size	Height Of Doll	Skin Fabric (doubled)	Fleece	Tube Gauze	or	Cotton Knit
A	20 cm. (8 in.)	20 x 20 cm. (8 x 8 in.)	100 g. (3.5 oz.)	20 cm. (8 in.)		10 x 10 cm. (4 x 4 in.)
B	30 cm. (12 in.)	30 x 30 cm. (12 x 12 in.)	200 g. (7 oz.)	30 cm. (12 in.)		15 x 15 cm. (6 x 6 in.)
C	40 cm. (16 in.)	40 x 40 cm. (16 x 16 in.)	300 g. (10.5 oz.)	40 cm. (16 in.)		20 x 20 cm. (8 x 8 in.)
D	50 cm. (20 in.)	50 x 50 cm. (20 x 20 in.)	400 g. (14 oz.)	50 cm. (20 in.)		25 x 25 cm. (10 x 10 in.)

It would be best to make sizes C and D in double-fabrics. You can line the doll with an inexpensive cotton knit (an old T-shirt). If you want to make a very thin doll, you can use a nonelastic cotton fabric for the lining. Use the same amount of lining fabric as skin fabric.

To make the doll:

Choose the size you want to make! Draw your own pattern on paper. As you notice, the pattern of the body is a rectangle. It's rounded on top for seam allowance, and on the bottom the legs are rounded off for the feet. See figure 28.

Draw the rectangle according to the measurements in table 2 below. Measure the length of the trunk and mark it off. Measure and mark the width of the thighs and the width of the toes. Connect these two marks, and you have the legs. The legs should look long since part of each of them is for a folded-up foot.

Table 2: Approximate body measurements of each doll in centimeters, with inches in parentheses. (Please don't take the fractions too seriously!)

Size	Full Height	Width	Trunk	Width of thigh	Toes
A	16	5	7.5	2.3	1.7
	(6¾)	(2)	(3)	(⅞)	(⅝)
B	24	7	11.3	3.2	2.3
	(9½)	(2¾)	(4½)	(1¼)	(⅞)
C	32	9	15	4	3
	(12¾)	(3½)	(6)	(1½)	(1⅛)
D	40	11	19	5	3.7
	(16)	(4 ¼)	(7½)	(2)	(1½)

When enlarging the patterns, for each centimeter that the doll's width increases, increase its height by four centimeters. If working with inches, increase the width one-quarter inch for each inch that you increase the height of the body.

Figure 29 shows suggested patterns for arms for each of the four sizes. The arms for sizes C and D must be lengthened. Draw the arm on transparent paper and put it over the drawing of the body. Make the arm as long as the trunk—see figure 28 and table 2!

The fabric for the head is a rectangle that measures twice the doll's width by just about the doll's full height. For size A, that's about 10 x 19 cm. (about 4 x 7 1/2 in.).

Note that fabrics can be more or less elastic. One type of knit fabric makes the doll thin, another may make it fat!

Transfer the pattern to the fabric

Figure 30 shows how the pattern pieces can be placed on

the fabric. Leave space for seam allowances of at least 0.5 cm. (1/4 in.) and for possible changes in length or width to adjust to the finished head size.

(To make sizes C and D more durable, make a lining. Use an inexpensive cotton knit and place it on the outside of the skin fabric so that you get four layers of fabric. Put lining fabric on the bottom, two layers of skin fabric in the middle, and then lining fabric again on the top. Draw the pattern onto the lining fabric. Once you've sewn together, cut out, and turned, the lining fabric ends up on the inside.)

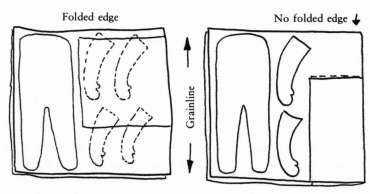

Fig. 30

Draw around the pattern with a ballpoint pen or a pencil. Hold the pieces of fabric together with some pins.

Next, make the head, before proceeding with the body. Once the head is made it can be held against the outline of the body and any adjustments in the body's size can be made to fit the finished head. But note that the body will end up a little shorter after it's sewn together and stuffed. See figure 47 (p. 148) for the proper proportions!

The head

Make the inner head out of the tube gauze. If you don't have tube gauze, you can use regular (not too thick!) cotton knit. See page 160 for the description of how to do it that way.

Twist the piece of tube gauze a couple of turns right in the middle and fold one half down over the other half to create a sack or pouch with double gauze. Or just tie a knot at one end with some rug warp and then turn the tube inside out so that the knot ends up inside.

Make a "star" of scoured fleece. Fairly long-fibered fleece works best. Put four gently twisted long strands of fleece on top of each other to form a star. Make a very firm ball of fleece—or use a ball of colorfast wool yarn—and put it in the center of the star. See figure 31a. Let the star embrace the ball so that you get a neck and shoulder area out of the "points" of the star.

Fig. 31a

Fig. 31b

Figure 31b shows you the resulting "jellyfish" of fleece. This is then stuffed into the tube-gauze pouch. See figure 32a.

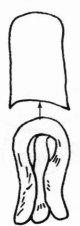

Fig. 32a

Fig. 32b

137

Gather the bottom of the pouch below the fleece and tie it up with rug warp. Now you have a somewhat large—and quite firm—head ball (fig. 32b).

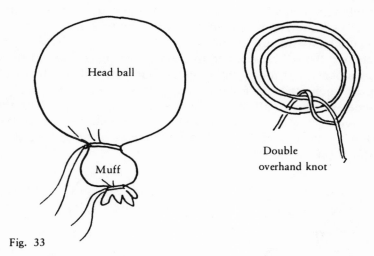

Head ball

Muff

Double
overhand knot

Fig. 33

Bind this off firmly for the neck by winding the rug warp twice around and tying a double overhand knot (fig. 33). Make sure that there's enough fleece in the muff below the neck. It should be fairly firm (fig. 34). Add more fleece if necessary.

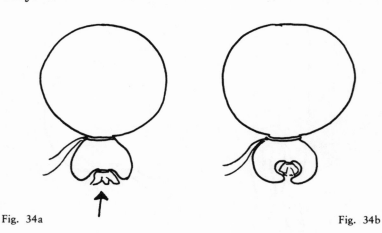

Fig. 34a   Fig. 34b

Press the loose-hanging fabric and the knot up into the muff. Using a darning needle and a strong thread, sew some large stitches at the bottom so that the pressed-up fabric is hidden (fig. 35).

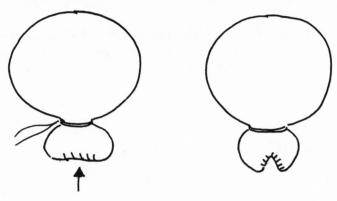

Fig. 35a   Front view   Side view   Fig. 35b

Again, push the stitches you've just sewn up into the muff, so that they also disappear. Sew new stitches at the bottom to make the muff smaller and flatter. The added width creates the "shoulders."

Now it's been decided which parts of the head will be its sides, for you don't want a shoulder sticking out of the chest! See figure 36.

Fig. 36

Front view. The muff has become smaller and firmer.

To test if the muff and the neck are sturdy enough, hold the muff in your hand with the head straight up and shake

139

it vigorously back and forth. If the head bends at the neck, it's too loose. In that case, undo the stitches and pack more fleece into it.

The muff should be no more than one-third as high as the head. It's the tension in the fabric at the neck that makes it sturdy.

(Another way of making the neck is described on page 160.)

Now look at the front and back of the head. Where is the best chin? By massaging the head, you can smooth out any uneven spots.

Binding off the inner head

Right in the middle of the head, wind rug warp twice around, tie a double overhand knot (fig. 33), and tighten firmly. See figure 37. You should get a good indentation. Tie a

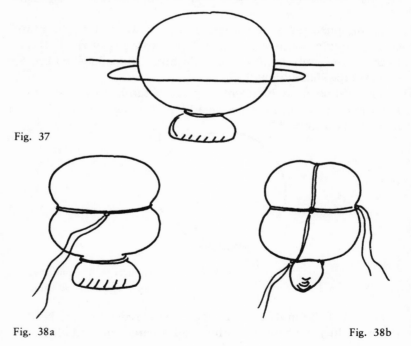

Fig. 37

Fig. 38a

Fig. 38b

knot. Move the knot to the back of the head. See figure 38.

If the head is stuffed too loosely, the warp will dig into it too deeply, almost "cutting it in two"! Restuff it in that case.

On the other hand, if you've stuffed the head too tightly, it will remain totally round no matter what you do. In that case, open it up and remove some fleece.

You have just put on the string for the eyes.

Now, wind doubled rug warp around the head at a right angle to the first string. Lay the warp over the crown and take it down to cross under the string for the eyes at a point where you can imagine the ears; pass the warp under and around the horizontal string, and then take it down under the chin and tie it in front of the neck. See figure 38b!

Stitch several stitches with a sewing thread at the crosses by the ears to attach the warp to the inner head.

To create a nicely rounded back of the head, push down on the rear section of the horizontal string, as in figure 39.

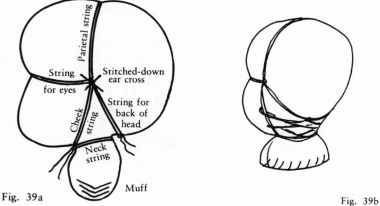

Fig. 39a

Fig. 39b

If the head shows a tendency towards having "mumps," you can massage the fleece forward to the cheeks or backward to the back of the head. You can make a neat nape of the neck with the two long string-ends hanging at the back of the neck: weave them back and forth between the cheek strings and the back-of-the head string and tie them up around the neck string. See figure 39b.

Tie an extra knot on each end and cut off the excess.

141

Skin fabric over the inner head

Turn the head piece of the skin fabric inside out and fold it double along the grain of the fabric (right sides facing). Put the inner head on the double fabric so that the face looks right at the folded edge. Draw a line along the back of the head and down to the muff. See figure 40! From the back of the head, the line goes straight up. Stitch twice with zigzag on the machine. Cut off excess fabric and turn.

(If you are sewing the doll with doubled fabric, even the head-fabric should be double. Put the lining fabric on the outside of the skin fabric when you draw and sew.)

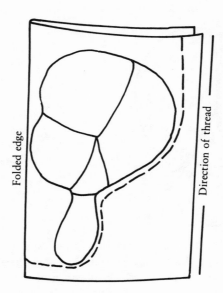

Fig. 40

Leaving the seam behind the head, pull the face fabric up over the head from below. Adjust the fabric so that the ribbing is vertical over the face. Pull the fabric up to cover the crown. Stitch by hand on top. See figure 41.

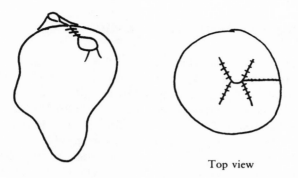

Top view

Fig. 41

Now pull the fabric downward below the muff to tighten it around the head. Tie a knot around the excess fabric under the muff. See figure 42.

Then tie a double overhand knot with rug warp under the chin—right outside the inner neck string. Stretching the fabric according to this method should make the chin and neck free of wrinkles.

You could also stitch up the skin fabric around the head entirely by hand, if you prefer. Keep the seams at the back and top of the head!

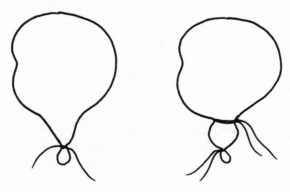

Fig. 42

Sewing the body and arms

After having adjusted the size of the body to fit the head (see p. 148 and fig. 47), it's time to stitch up the body and arms. Use a very light zigzag stitch and sewing machine needle no. 70 (European size; or U.S. size 10–12). Stitch right on the line before you actually cut out the pieces (to avoid the fabric's being pulled into the machine, as will happen if the seam is close to the edge of the fabric). Leave the top of the body sides unstitched, to give room for the arms. Leave the top of the arms open. See figure 43. Stitch twice, making the second seam just outside the first. If you don't have a zigzag stitch on your machine, a straight stitch will also work.

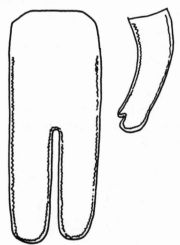

Fig. 43

Cut out the pieces and trim off all excess fabric! In the crotch between the legs, and also between the thumb and the hand, you have to cut close to the seam in order to be able to turn the fabric.

(If you want to make a baby doll with bent legs, try the following variation. After you've trimmed off the excess fabric, make a few folds on the insides and backs of the legs, about halfway down. Sew them up by machine: the legs will curl inwards and back. See also page 164, figure 67.)

Turn the body and the arms, poke out the thumbs.

Stuffing the body and arms

Prepare two equal-sized wads of fleece for the feet. Stuff the wads down into the feet and pin a straight pin right across, so that you create a fleece-free space between the feet and legs (fig. 44a).

Prepare two good-sized fleece "clouds" for the legs. Fold up a leg as you do when preparing to put on a sock. Take fluffy wads, one after the other, and press them down into the leg so that you make something like a stack of bowls, one on top of the other (fig. 44b).

Fig. 44a

Fig. 44b

When the legs are firmly stuffed (the doll should be able to stand!), put straight pins across the top.

Make a big roll of fleece for the body. The more firmly the doll is stuffed, the longer it holds its shape and the easier it is to dress and undress.

Stuff fleece into the arms, but leave the top thirds empty. Put in straight pins to keep the fleece from slipping out. See figure 45 on next page.

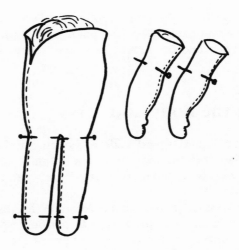

Fig. 45

Fig. 46

Timothy is 30 cm. (nearly 12 in.), sewn according to the description of the dress-up doll (size B). He has been washed by machine several times, but—please note!—without letting the children watch! Whirling around in the spin cycle is a terrifying thought.

Assembly and proportions

Compare the two stuffed arms. Are they stuffed so as to be equally firm? Feel also to see if the legs are alike.

When putting the doll together, you have to keep the proportions in mind: the head is to be one-fourth of the total height of the doll.

The legs and the trunk end up being about the same length once the seam allowance on top is folded down and the feet are folded up. The arms should be shorter than the legs, and should reach to the groin. Children's heads are relatively large. The navel is midway between the head and the feet.

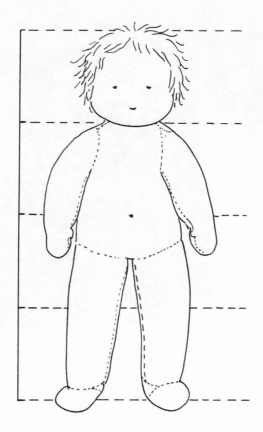

Fig. 47

Remove the pins from the arms and put them together as in figure 48. Make them overlap a bit, with the arm-seams in the midline. The thumbs should be pointing in the same direction! Sew the arms together.

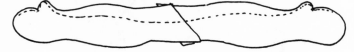

Fig. 48

With a few large stitches, attach the sewn-together arms to the back of the muff. See figure 49. If the muff then seems to bulge out too much, you can sew a few times right through the muff from front to back: pull tight, using a large darning needle and strong thread. This technique will flatten the muff.

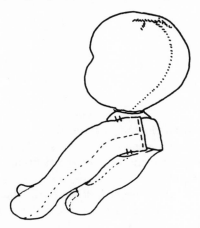

Fig. 49

Choose which side will make the best stomach-side of the body, and then insert the head and arms appropriately. See figure 50a on next page.

Fold down the front seam allowance around the fleece and pin the fabric to the neck right under the chin. Then fold down the back fabric more than the front and attach it, too, with a pin. The back fabric needs to be tauter than the front to give the doll a straight back and a rounded stomach (fig. 50b).

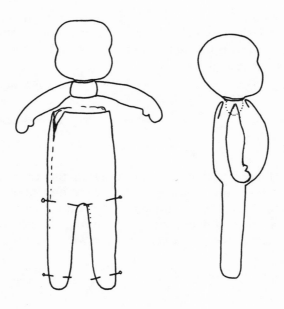

Fig. 50a   Fig. 50b

Sewing with doubled thread, attach the body fabric to the neck. If it's too hard a reach to make small stitches, you can sew longer stitches and sew several turns around the neck to create a tight seam.

Next, sew the shoulder seams down from the neck. Fold in more of the shoulder seam allowance at the far end, so that you create slightly sloping shoulders.

If the openings for the arms now seem too large, first sew up some of each side seam of the body to make smaller armholes. Fold the fabric in around each armhole. Make sure that the thumb is pointing diagonally forward, and then sew on each arm. The smaller the armhole is, the more durable it will be. A smaller armhole also allows the arm to be more mobile and to hang down more nicely.

Now the doll is sewn together, but there are still some details left.

Stitched-off legs, feet, etc.

Stitched-off legs

To enable the doll to sit and to keep the fleece in the legs, hand-sew a diagonal seam up and out from the crotch. Stitch back and forth. It's easier to get the same angle on both seams if you start at the outside and stitch in towards the crotch. See figure 47.

The feet

Remove the pins at the feet and fold the foot up at a right angle towards the front of the leg. Attach the foot to the leg by sewing twice across. Using a strong thread, sew a gathering seam around each ankle; tighten it a little to give the doll daintier feet and something of a heel.

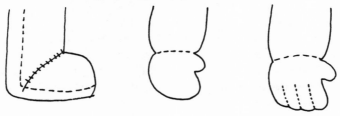

Fig. 51

Wrists

Using a strong thread, stitch a gathering seam around the wrist, pull it tight, and stitch down. This gives the hand a more childlike, chubby appearance. On the smallest doll, you can sew a gathering seam just on the inside of the wrist.

Fingers

Fingers are really not necessary!
Start with the seam in the middle and then divide each of the two sides again with a seam. Start in the hand and sew out to the fingertips. Note that sewing fingers widens the

151

hand. If it seems quite wide already, you can take in the side first.

Toes

Sew them like the fingers. They can look all right on the large baby-sized doll, but they usually don't come out well.

Navel

Sew a small pink dot with sewing thread.

The face

Nose

A nose is really not necessary! It tends to get dirty very quickly. If you still want to make one, you can make a tiny little ball of fleece and sew it onto the inner head before the skin fabric is put on. It's very difficult to place it right and even more difficult to place the eyes and mouth at equal distances from the nose.

Eyes

Test with straight pins to see where the eyes and mouth should be. (See p. 174 for the most common mistakes made when sewing the doll.) The eyes are sewn on top of the eyestring. Try to stitch them around the string.

Use a long and thin darning needle that you can insert into the head somewhere far away from the eye—preferably back where the hair will be. See figure 52.

Sew one eye. Use thin woolen thread—for example, darning thread. Count the number of stitches for the first eye, so that you can repeat the same number for the second eye. Stitch from one eye to the next and sew it, then bring the needle out at the back of the head again. The thread you use

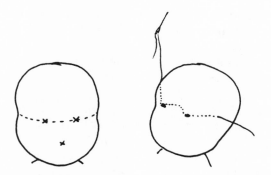

Fig. 52

for the eyes will be held by the fleece inside the head, so you don't have to fasten the thread-ends.

Mouth

The mouth is placed below the eyes so that the three dots form an equilateral triangle. A shiny, pink thread is good, but slippery thread might eventually slip out. Sew very small stitches close together for a small mouth.

If you have a needle that is long enough, you can fasten the thread at the back of the neck, stitch forward to the mouth, sew it, and then return to the back of the neck and fasten the thread again.

Cheeks

You can make red cheeks with a wax crayon to give the doll a healthy look. The color wears off surprisingly fast— a comfort to those who have used too much!

Now the doll itself has been "born." Please don't be tempted to sew in all kinds of creases, genitals, hips, and whatever else! The child will use its own imagination to give the doll all the characteristics it desires!

The hair

Let your imagination flow! But remember that the doll

153

looks prettiest with thin hair that emphasizes the shape of the head, and that it is primarily the hairline that gives a doll its special character.

Blending two similar color tones gives life to the hair! Or why not use natural dyes like onion skins, walnut hulls, alder bark, and eucalyptus leaves?

You can make the yarn curly by knitting with it, wetting it, and then letting it dry before unravelling it again.

If you can get thick yarn through the skin-fabric, you can make the hair quickly. But it doesn't turn out very nice: it gaps easily, and it looks unnaturally large. The doll can hardly get its cap on.

Synthetic yarns don't give the same natural lustre as wool; they look dead in comparison.

If you want to use cotton yarn for the hair, try to find a thin cotton weaving yarn. The cotton yarns made for knitting and crocheting wear out and eventually break.

Fig. 53

Hairstyles

1. Smooth, embroidered hair

Sew a row of large stitches parallel to one another around

the whole hairline. Keep filling in with stitches around and around, converging towards a point in the middle of the scalp, until the whole scalp is covered. See figure 54!

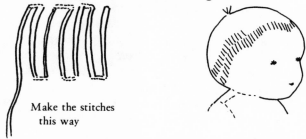

Make the stitches
this way

Fig. 54

This technique makes a very durable hairdo suitable for younger children. They can't pull it off.

You can add thin bangs with loose ends, and a tuft of hair on top. To give a slightly fuzzy finish, cut open a few of the stitches, or sew on short loose-ends afterwards.

Another, less orderly, short hairdo can be made by sewing a large "darning patch" over the scalp. Sew very large stitches right across half of the head; go first in one direction, then in the other, weaving up and down through the first stitches as if you were darning socks. Leave yarn ends here and there to make the doll pleasantly unkempt!

2. Curly hair

Alternatives:

Make a long fringe or a very loosely crocheted band and

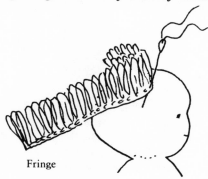

Fig. 55   Fringe

stitch it onto the scalp in a tight spiral. Start at the outside and move in towards the middle, or work in the opposite direction!

Or crochet a loose cap and sew it onto the head. Pull up loops here and there from the loose crocheting.

Unravel something knitted and make a large "mess" of yarn. Lay it on the head and stitch it on in a spiral; use sewing thread, and be very thorough. Sew methodically, so that the hair doesn't end up hanging loose or coming off.

Or, if you want to spend more time and get the most durable alternative, sew little loops all over the head, very close together!

3. Small, firm braids

This hairdo brings out the shape of the head and looks real. Sew a smooth hairdo as in the first hairstyle, but lay the stitches so as to create a part in the middle. Leave long ends here and there around the ears—see figure 56—which then can be braided into two cute pigtails. A fuzzy mohair yarn is very good.

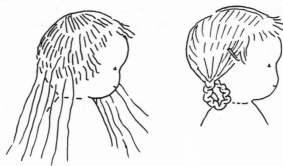

Fig. 56

4. Hanging hair without bangs

Lay a thick layer of yarn across the head—see figure 57. Decide how long the doll's hair should be, adjust the yarn, and cut it to the chosen length. To keep the yarn in place

156

while you're sewing it on, put a rubber band around the hair and head over the eye thread. Sew a part in the middle by backstitching to about where the head starts to slope downwards in the back. Using small stitches, sew back again along the part: the smaller you make the stitches, the more durable the hair will be.

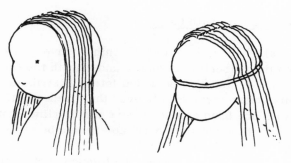

Fig. 57

Spread the hair to cover the back of the head. Remove the rubber band and sew a seam with small stitches from temple to temple around the back of the head where the rubber band was (see fig. 58). Make sure that the hair on the crown is smooth. Use a wide-toothed comb to comb it. Now stitch a few long stitches on the smooth hair on the crown (to prevent future gaps from appearing). Next, fold up all the hair

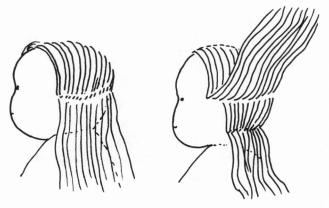

Fig. 58

at the nape of the neck (see fig. 58), let a thin layer of it
back down, and then stitch it to the back of the head as the
bottom hairline—take care that the doll should be able to hear!

If the hair is thick enough, you can make several layers
and seams above the bottom one.

Smooth out and style the hair!

5. Hanging hair with bangs

To make bangs, first place a thin layer of yarn that goes
in the other direction to and is underneath the thicker top
layer of hair that will be added later. Distribute the yarn
for this under-layer evenly over the forehead. Hold onto the
hair with one hand and see where the hairline should be. Sew
a seam right across the hairline—remember that children
usually have high foreheads!

Sew several seams across the top and back of the head that
are parallel to the first—all the way down to the back of the
neck. See figure 59! Now place the top layer of hair and
sew it on as shown in the previous description. Even it out
so that it looks like number 5 in figure 53.

Fig. 59

6. "Shag"

Those who like to work on something that takes time can
sew "rya knots" (hooks) over the whole head, close together,
and then cut open the hooks.

If you first sew a layer of hair underneath, as in hairstyle
5, the process will go a little more quickly. Place a thin but

158

dense layer of hair with bangs in the front. Attach it with transverse seams. Cut the hair off at the neck.

Continue placing this bottom layer of hair down the sides of the head and around the imagined ear, as in figure 59. Then systematically sew loops about every centimeter (approx. 3/8 in.) across the whole bottom hair. Start in the middle, for instance, and slowly work your way outwards. If you hold one hand over the already-finished loops, they won't follow and get stuck with each stitch you make.

Fig. 60

You don't have to sew "rya knots"—it's enough to stitch one stitch down into the head between each loop. Cut open the loops and even out. The longer the loops are, the thicker the hair looks.

Sometimes the yarn keeps breaking off as you're sewing the loops. Maybe the eye of the needle is too sharp? Try another needle. Sew with short ends. Don't try to gain time by using quadrupled thread, because the threads won't go through the skin.

The hair can also be attached with regular sewing thread of the same color, if the hair is made of cotton or mohair. But straight woolen hair easily slips out of the regular thread stitches.

Now the doll is finished! Does it look like you?

Other ways to make the doll

The neck

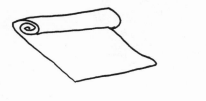

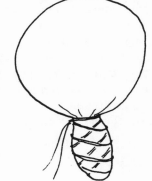

Fig. 61

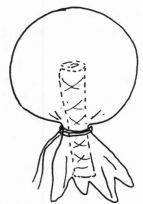

Fig. 62

Instead of making a muff, you can make a hard roll out of
a piece of bedsheet. Simply roll it up tightly. Then wind rug
warp tightly around it and use it as a core for the neck. There
is then no muff under the head. Instead, you get a cylinder-
like neck which can be inserted into the loose fabric below
the head and wound up. This type of neck is better if you have
no long-fibered fleece. See figures 61 and 62!

The inner head

Instead of using tube gauze for the inner head, you can use
regular cotton knit. To keep the head ball from being all
wrinkled, we sew an inner pouch, as wide as the doll's body
and no longer than the doll's trunk. (The measurements are
listed in table 2, p. 135.) The star of fleece is stuffed into
this pouch, which will then enclose the fleece ball. See figure 63.

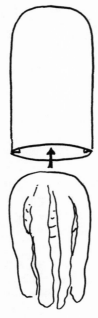

Fig. 63

Sew up the pouch at the bottom, tie off for the neck, press up the bottom stitches into the muff as described on page 139, and sew up to make the muff hard.

The side seams on the pouch must be placed at the sides of the head—otherwise they will show through the skin fabric. Compare with figures 64 and 65!

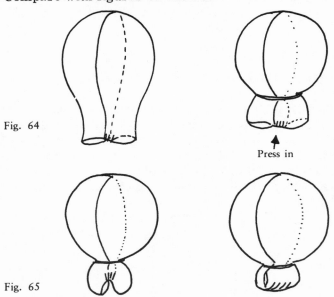

Fig. 64

Press in

Fig. 65

The body

The body can be made out of a rolled-up wool sweater.

Cut off the sleeves of the sweater and roll it up minus the sleeves. See if the body fits the size of the finished head. Insert the roll into one of the sweater sleeves and sew with large stitches to make a package. Leave a hole in the roll for the neck. Sew up the package at the top; attach the head by stitching right through the neck if possible.

Now there's no muff to attach the sleeves to. So, split the top third of the arm into two parts and attach it to the body as shown in figure 66!

Stuff fleece into the legs, stitch the groin seams, and pull on the body fabric. Sew up around the neck, at the shoulders, and, finally, around the arms.

This method makes a heavy and sturdy doll, but it takes longer to dry after being washed than fleece-filled ones do.

Fig. 66

If you don't have access to fleece, the doll can be stuffed with rolled-up pieces of a sweater.

The legs

The legs can be sewn individually and then attached to the body. Draw your own pattern of two legs in profile, plus two soles of the feet. See figure 67 on next page!

These bent legs keep their shape better than the ones made by just sewing a fold at the back of the knee, but they are harder for a beginner to sew.

It's a good idea to first sew a sample out of an old under-shirt, so that you can see how the legs will turn out.

When you've arrived at a good pattern, transfer it to the

163

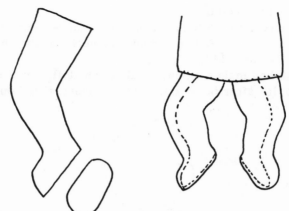

Fig. 67

fabric, stitch twice with a faint zigzag stitch, cut off excess fabric, and sew on the soles of the feet. Turn, and stuff firmly with fleece. Stitch up the legs across the top so that the leg-seams are in the front and the back. Attach the legs to the body fabric. Stuff the body and continue as in the regular description.

Fig. 68

Maya from the cover photo is 40 cm. (15¾ in.) tall and has boots and a hat made out of chamois cloth. Children often like unusually frilly clothes: they're considered fancy. It's fun if the doll gets clothes similar to the child's own.

Clothes

Dolls can catch colds, too! Don't leave them all naked in a drafty corner of the room.

When sewing doll clothes, it's important to think about the age of the child who will use them.

A two-year-old can have a doll with clothes that are attached.

A three-year-old will most likely want to pull the doll's clothes off. Therefore, sew them in a durable material, and with simple fasteners—elastic, or large buttons.

The four-year-old can manage zippers, and the six-year-old can usually tie a bow.

The clothes should be sufficiently large.

The snowsuit should be made large enough to fit over whatever else the doll may be wearing!

Use simple, sturdy fabrics, plain or small-patterned and in light, cheerful colors—no dreary, murky colors! Cotton, wool, flannel, felt, velour, and terry cloth are good.

A popular activity for doll parents is to arrange a big laundry day for the doll clothes.

Some ideas for simple clothes

1. Tunic or dress

Measure the distance between the doll's hands, and the distance from the chin to where the tunic or dress will end. Allow margins for seam allowances, and then, on doubled fabric, cut out a rectangle with those measurements. Leaving a large opening for the neck, sew together the tops of

Fig. 69

the sleeves.

Stitch down the edge of neckline to make a narrow space for a thin elastic band. Cut in below the sleeves, and diagonally down (see fig. 69), and then stitch up the sleeves and the sides. Turn and try it on the doll to see how long the sleeves and the dress should be. Hem, and insert elastic at neck.

2. Dress sewn in straight pieces

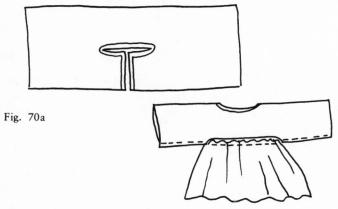

Fig. 70a

Fig. 70b

Measure the distance from wrist-to-wrist when the doll's arm's are outstretched, and from the chin to a point just

beyond the reach of the doll's lowered arms.

Cut out a piece with the above measurements on folded fabric—the fold should be horizontal and will form the top of the sleeves. Now fold the piece vertically in the middle and cut out the neckhole. Open the vertical fold and cut up mid-front or mid-back. Edge the opening with bias tape, and stitch up the sleeves. Measure where you want the button. See figure 70a!

Now take another (long) piece of fabric for the skirt and sew a gathering stitch at the top. Adjust to fit around the doll. Pin the fabric to the top piece, right sides together, and stitch. Sew up the skirt in the back, or leave a little opening by sewing on the bias tape. Hem the skirt. See figure 70b!

3. Slacks

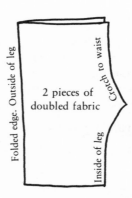

Fig. 71

Measure the doll around its waist, and from the waist to the foot. Add a little in the width. Cut out two doubled pieces with a folded edge along the sides. The folded edges will make the outsides of the legs. Pin a straight pin in the middle of the cut side, and cut out the curves. The pin marks the the crotch.

Since the dolls' bodies are quite round, slacks must be rather high-waisted so that they don't slip down.

Stitch up the legs. Pin the two pieces right sides together, sew the seam from the waist to the crotch, and then sew up to the waist again in the back. Fold down for a waistband

168

and put in elastic. Hem the legs.

4. Underpants

Measure a little more than double the waist of the doll.
Measure from the high waist to the crotch. Cut a rectangle
with these measurements on doubled fabric and sew up the
sides. Fold down at the waist and up at the bottom edge;
put in elastic both at the waist and at the bottom. Sew a few
stitches between the legs.

Fig. 72

A cut-off sleeve from an old undershirt or the cuff of an
old sock can be used for underpants. Hem the cut-off end,
stitch between the legs, and it's finished.

5. Tights

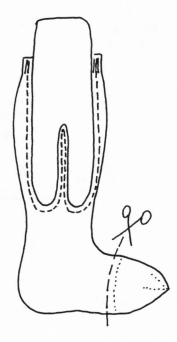

Fig. 73

169

Place the pattern you used for the doll on an old wool knee-sock, or on a piece of tricot. Draw a bit beyond the outline, and stitch with a zigzag seam. Cut off excess fabric, and turn. If you've used a sock, there's already elastic at the top; if not, put in an elastic band.

6. <u>Hat or cap</u>

Crochet around and around for a beret. Start by single-crocheting as many stitches as you need to fit around the head. Add some extra stitches, because the beret will tend to shrink as you crochet the next row. Skipping stitches here and there to reduce the size, crochet around and around towards the middle.

You can make a little bonnet out of a long and narrow piece of fabric. Measure the distance from ear to ear over the head, and from the ear to the back of the neck. Cut out a rectangle with these measurements. Round off the front corners. Place the fabric over the doll's head and fold it down over the ears. Put the bottom edges together in the back and fold down a flap of the top part of the seam in the back. Pin together, take the bonnet off, and stitch up the flap seam. Edge with bias tape and attach a button or use bands for tying with.

7. <u>Boots</u>

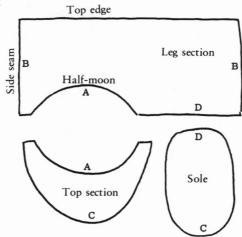

Fig. 74

Measure the circumference of the leg above the foot. Draw
a rectangle with this measurement as the long side, and the
desired height of the bootleg as the short side. Cut out in
doubled fabric. Draw a half-moon big enough to cover the
top of the foot, add seam allowances, and cut out in doubled
fabric.

Draw and cut out a sole the same size as the underside of
the foot, plus seam allowances. Cut a half-moon into one of
the bootleg's long sides, as shown in figure 74. Sew together
according to the letters in figure 74, so that the half-moon
on the bootleg meets the section designed for the top of the
foot as shown. Sew up the side seam on the bootleg. Finally,
stitch on the sole underneath. Suitable fabrics are either
felt or chamois cloth. Sew with large stitches to avoid making the boot too detailed. Compare with figure 68 on page 165.

8. Hooded sweater

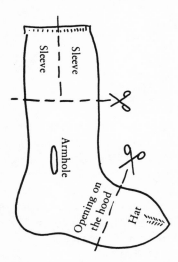

Fig. 75

The doll pictured on page 71 has a sweater made from a
sock. The toe of the sock makes a hat, and the heel makes
a hood. Cut two holes in the sides for the sleeves, and cut
enough material for two sleeves out of the rest of the sock.
Stitch up the two sleeves and sew them into the armholes.
Fold and carefully hem all cut edges. If the sock is long
enough, there might also be enough material for pants.

Advice for washing

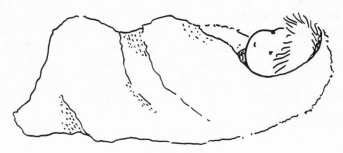

Fig. 76

Normal soiling

Rub soap and lukewarm water with a sponge or nailbrush on the soiled spots. Dry by trying to soak up as much of the water as possible into a towel pressed firmly against the doll. Place the doll in a high place to dry—but not over a hot heater! Wool, as is well known, can't tolerate temperatures much over 30° C. (86° F.) without becoming felted. Washing water should be skin temperature at most. Large differences in temperatures, hard scrubbing, and synthetic detergents cause the fine spirals in the wool's fibers to stiffen and break. The wool looses its elasticity, becomes rigid.

Heavy soiling

All of the dolls in this book can be washed by machine on the gentle cycle with only short spinning. Use only pure soap!

Dry the doll by wrapping it in a bath towel and placing it in a high place in the room. Let it sit comfortably, for it takes at least two days for the larger dolls to dry.

It's preferable not to show the children how the doll is churned around in the machine. The thought that the doll is spinning around in there can frighten or disturb them.

The child bathes the doll

Yes, the doll can be bathed. But you should explain to the child that it takes a very long time to dry, particularly if it's not spun in the machine. The child can rub soap into the doll and then squeeze it to let the soapy water run through it.

Stay near by when the child is about to remove the doll from the water, as floods of water will soon come pouring out of it.

Before the doll is wrapped up in a towel to dry, you must check that it has kept its shape. The legs, body, and arms may shorten and thicken. In that case, squeeze it gently and pull on it carefully to restore its original shape.

Repairs and adjustments

Never let a damaged doll remain with the child. It is "sick" and therefore needs care.

If you neglect this care, a child with a lively imagination might worry that you also wouldn't notice if he were sick.

A broken doll doesn't make a very good impression on the child, either—especially not if it's the favorite doll.

Ten common mistakes

1. The doll is stuffed too loosely

The legs buckle in the wrong direction when the doll is stood up. You can feel right through the stomach when you press it.

What to do: Open up holes in the side seams, or under the arms, and stuff in more fleece. If the old fleece is lying all lumpy at the bottom of the legs, you can take it out and card it or pull it apart to fluff it up. Restuff the doll.

2. The arms are different lengths or too long

Measure the lengths of the arms by holding them along the sides: the thumbs should reach to about the groin seam. Better too short than too long!

What to do: Shorten an arm by the following method. First, take out the seam where the arm attaches to the body. Then, tie rug warp tightly around the arm at the point where it should end. Press the excess piece of the arm into the body and stitch the armhole again, just under the rug warp.

174

3. Shoulders have different widths

More fabric was allowed to one side of the neck than to the other.

What to do: Find the vertical midline of the body fabric by following the ribbing straight up from the crotch to the chin. If the midline has ended up shifted to one side, the neck seam must be undone.

Then make sure the midline ends up right under the chin and restitch the body fabric to the neck.

4. The doll is hunchbacked

Fig. 77

The fabric wasn't pulled tightly enough at the back, or the muff is too thick.

What to do: If the muff is too thick, the doll needs to be ripped open to bare the muff. To flatten it, sew a few strong stitches back and forth between the front and the back of the muff. If the back fabric hasn't been stretched well enough, you don't need to rip open the seam. Just make a good fold in the back fabric, turn it up towards the neck, and stitch it to the neck above the old seam.

5. The head looks crooked

The doll turns its head to one side. The problem is most likely that the arms have been attached crookedly to the muff.

What to do: This problem is hard to correct without ripping out and replacing the arms correctly on the muff. But try to rip out only the stitching around the neck, and then turn the head to the correct position before restitching.

6. The face is crooked on the head

Maybe even the hair is not symmetrical on the head.

What to do: Carefully cut open the eyes and mouth with small scissors. Mark for new eyes with straight pins. If you hold the doll at a little distance, or look at it in a mirror, it will be easier for you to see if something is crooked. The doll should look straight ahead. Try to form an equilateral triangle with the dots in the face. See figure 78.

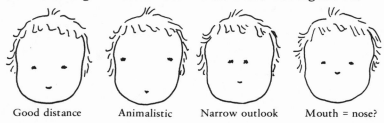

| Good distance | Animalistic | Narrow outlook | Mouth = nose? |

Fig. 78

Place the eyes on the eye line. But if the string for the eyes on the inner head is crooked, you first have to massage fleece under the string to move it to the right position. Sew on new dots.

If you wet the holes left from the old dots, the fabric will pull together. If the hairline has been sewn too far down into parts of the face where there shouldn't be any hair, you can cut open those stitches also, and wet the remaining holes.

A high forehead gives the doll a dainty and childish expression.

7. Holes and runs along the machine stitch

Too large a needle has been used. Certain cotton knits can only handle a very thin sewing machine needle. European size 70 or U. S. sizes 10–12 are recommended.

What to do: Sew up the seam by hand so that the holes are totally hidden. Hand sewn seams usually last longer than the machine-stitched ones.

8. Legs too short

Are the legs shorter than the body? Are the feet too big?

What to do: If you've folded up feet that are too big, just rip out the stitching, fold up smaller feet, and the legs will lengthen.

If the legs are too short even with feet of a minimal size, one of two things could be the cause. You may have stuffed them too hard, so that they became too thick and shortened, or your pattern may have been too short. Then you can sew new little feet to attach at the bottom of the legs. First rip out the stitches and fold the old feet down. Make two more feet according to the pattern for feet, but allow about five more centimeters (approx. 2 in.) to the doll's legs. Sew up the feet, cut off excess fabric, and turn. Stuff fleece into the little pouches. Fold down the upper edge more than the bottom edge, attach to the legs with pins, and sew fast. Remove pins.

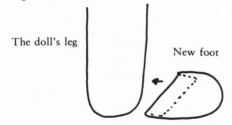

The doll's leg

New foot

Fig. 79

9. The fleece creeps out of the fabric

Fleece has mysterious ways: sometimes it creeps out, sometimes it doesn't, even with the same fabric.

What to do: Shave the doll with a razor! Don't pull out the threads—new ones follow forever and ever! If it's really bad, you might have to cover the doll with more fabric on top of the old. The fleece won't come out through doubled fabric.

10. The hair is too thin

The scalp shows through.

What to do: It's easy to embroider on some extra hair-yarn, if you have some left over. Or, you can use a yarn similar to the hair. Sew with long stitches in the direction of the hair so that the gaps are filled in, or sew a new layer on top of the old. Balding dolls look pretty pathetic, don't they?

When the beloved doll is hopelessly worn out

The fabric falls apart, the fleece shows through the hands and feet—but the child can't imagine giving up the favorite doll?

You can suggest that the doll be taken to the hospital for a while. If that's all right, prepare the child for the fact that the doll might not look exactly the same when it comes back.

In the first stage, you can sew a totally new body, make new arms and legs, rip open the seams of the old doll, take out the fleece, and pull it or card it to fluff it up. Then stuff the new body and put the old head onto it.

Then the doll gets to come home from the hospital for a while. It's still the child's dear old doll, even though the body is new.

But later, when the head has to be repaired, it's hospital-time again. If the hair is still good and strong, you can re-cover the old face with new fabric, sew new eyes and a new mouth, and sew a hidden seam all around right at the hair-line.

The doll is not too different after this plastic surgery!

If it's really necessary, the doll gets a new head. Throw away the leftovers of the old one, so that the child won't see them! Buy new yarn for the hair that is as similar in quality and color to the old hair as possible.

The doll gets to come home again, and now it's totally new. But for the child, it's still the well-known favorite.

Not all children will get so attached to a certain doll. Naturally, a new doll could replace the worn-out one. It could, perhaps, be a slightly more advanced model, since the child is older. Perhaps a smaller doll, instead of the big one that the child has had for many years, would be just right.

Better Than School

Nancy Wallace

Introduction by John Holt

One family's
declaration of independence

Education/Parenting
256 pages   5½ x 8½   Illustrated
0-943914-05-1   Smyth-sewn
$14.95 cloth

"I felt from the beginning that this would be a very
valuable book to have in print and I am more pleased
than I can say that it has now appeared....no other
book I have read takes us so deeply into the day-to-
day thoughts and concerns of a parent, or the day-to-
day lives of parents with their children. More than any
other book about home-schooling, this tells us what
the experience of home-schooling was actually like, in
one family at least....enjoy and learn from this lovely
book. What the Wallaces (and many others) have
done, you and your children—if you want to—can also
do."

—John Holt, from the introduction

What can be done when 'compulsory attendance' regulations actually *interfere* with a child's learning process? Nancy and Bob Wallace have developed one answer that works.

After a year of watching their bright, talented, and sensitive son grow more miserable by the day in school, Nancy and Bob Wallace withdrew him from school to experiment with home-based education on their own. Their daughter (who has never been to school) soon chose to be the second member of their "school-at-home."

Their success is a story for anyone interested in how children learn and in how to strengthen and enjoy adult-child relationships. Healthy, happy, and well ahead of their "grade levels," the Wallace children are proof that at least some children need neither a formal school environment nor adult pressure in order to learn, to create, and to grow into responsible human beings.

Why the Wallaces felt forced to take this radical alternative, how they convinced their school administrators to recognize their right to do so, how they have modernized the ideal of the family unit in response to their children's educational needs, and what other parents and many educators can learn from the Wallaces' experiences are the main themes of *Better Than School*.

Legal struggles on the controversial issue of home-schooling are underway throughout the country. Should school systems oppose or support and cooperate with this rapidly expanding movement? After reading *Better Than School*, you will be much more informed on what is involved in this thoroughly American alternative.

Distributed exclusively to the book trade by Kampmann & Company, 9 East 40 St., New York, NY 10016. Schools, libraries, associations, and individuals may also order direct from Larson Publications, 4936 Route 414, Box 79A, Burdett, NY 14818.

- *"Who can remember when the times were not hard and money not scarce?"*
  —Emerson

- *"A book that everyone should read, because it affects all of us....Rich or poor, this fascinating volume packs a load of material for all to consider. "*
  —Sid Ascher, Sid Ascher's World

- *"Cut the fluff out of your life...you'll also be more able to see what's really important...self-discipline is the key to staying within predetermined limits. "*
  —Fritchman/Solomon

Consumer Education
Finance, Personal
Practical Guides

224 pages

5½ x 8½

Illustrated

0-943914-03-5

Smyth-sewn

$8.95, paper

Self-sufficiency and self-respect in hard times as well as good ones are the basic themes of *Living Lean*. A cheerful philosophy of thrift without stinginess, with many witty strategies for living comfortably on little income. Covers food, clothing, housing, child rearing, money management, and survival. Extensive selection of recipes and craft ideas. Good for students.

Distributed exclusively to the book trade by Kampmann & Company, 9 East 40 St., New York, NY 10016. Schools, libraries, associations, individuals, and non-booktrade retailers may also order direct from Larson Publications, 4936 Route 414, Box 79A, Burdett, NY 14818.